So Good They Can't Ignore You

So Good They Can't Ignore You

Why Skills Trump Passion in the Quest for Work You Love

CAL NEWPORT

GRAND CENTRAL
PUBLISHING

NEW YORK   BOSTON

Grand Central Publishing
Hachette Book Group
1290 Avenue of the Americas
New York, NY 10104

www.HachetteBookGroup.com

Printed in the United States of America
RRD-C

First Edition: September 2012
10   9

Grand Central Publishing is a division of Hachette Book Group, Inc.
The Grand Central Publishing name and logo are trademarks of Hachette Book Group, Inc.

The Hachette Speakers Bureau provides a wide range of authors for speaking events. To find out more, go to www.hachettespeakersbureau.com or call (866) 376-6591.

The publisher is not responsible for websites (or their content) that are not owned by the publisher.

Library of Congress Cataloging-in-Publication Data

Newport, Cal.
So good they can't ignore you: why skills trump passion in the quest for work you love / Cal Newport.—1st ed.
p. cm.
ISBN 978-1-4555-0912-6
1. Vocational guidance.   2. Personality and occupation.   I. Title.
HF5381.N497 2012
650.1—dc23
2011045291

To Julie

Contents

Introduction

The Passion of the Monk

"'Follow your passion' is dangerous advice."

Thomas had this realization in one of the last places you might expect. He was walking a trail through the oak forest that outlines the southern bowl of Tremper Mountain. The trail was one of many that cross through the 230-acre property of the Zen Mountain Monastery, which has called this corner of the Catskill Mountains its home since the early 1980s. Thomas was halfway through a two-year stay at the monastery, where he was a practicing lay monk. His arrival, one year earlier, had been the fulfillment of a dream-job fantasy that he had nurtured for years. He had followed his passion for all things Zen into this secluded Catskills retreat and had expected happiness in return. As he stood in the oak forest that afternoon, however, he began to cry, his fantasy crumbling around him.

"I was always asking, 'What's the meaning of life?'" Thomas told me when I first met him, at a coffee shop in Cambridge, Massachusetts. By then, several years had passed since Thomas's realization in the Catskills, but the path that led him to that point remained clear and he was eager to talk about it, as if the recounting would help exorcise the demons of his complicated past.

After earning a pair of bachelor's degrees in philosophy and theology, then a master's degree in comparative religion, Thomas decided that Zen Buddhist practice was the key to a meaningful life. "There was such a big crossover between the philosophy I was studying and Buddhism that I thought, 'Let me just go practice Buddhism directly to answer these big questions,'" he told me.

After graduation, however, Thomas needed money, so he took on a variety of jobs. He spent a year, for example, teaching English in Gumi, an industrial town in central South Korea. To many, life in East Asia might sound romantic, but this exoticism soon wore off for Thomas. "Every Friday night, after work, the men would gather at these street carts, which had tents extending out from them," Thomas told me. "They gathered to drink soju [a distilled rice liquor] late into the night. During winter there would be steam coming from these tents, from all the men drinking. What I remember most, however, is that the next morning the streets would be covered in dry vomit."

Thomas's search also inspired him to travel across China and into Tibet, and to spend time in South Africa, among other journeys, before ending up in London working a rather dull job in data entry. Throughout this period, Thomas nurtured his conviction that Buddhism held the key to his happiness. Over time, this daydream evolved into the idea of him living as a monk. "I had built up such an incredible fantasy about Zen practice and living in a Zen monastery," he explained to me. "It came to represent my dream come true." All other work paled in comparison to this fantasy. He was dedicated to following his passion.

It was while in London that Thomas first learned about the Zen Mountain Monastery, and he was immediately attracted to its seriousness. "These people were practicing really intense and sincere Zen," he recalls. His passion insisted that the Zen Mountain Monastery was where he belonged.

It took nine months for Thomas to complete the application process. When he finally arrived at Kennedy airport, having been approved to come live and practice at the monastery, he boarded a bus to take him into the Catskill countryside. The ride took three hours. After leaving the city sprawl, the bus proceeded through a series of quaint towns, with the scenery getting "progressively more beautiful." In a scene of almost contrived symbolism, the bus eventually reached the foot of Tremper Mountain, where it stopped and let Thomas out at a crossroads. He walked from the bus stop down the road leading to the monastery entrance, which was guarded by a pair of wrought-iron gates, left open for new arrivals.

Once on the grounds, Thomas approached the main building, a four-story converted church constructed from local bluestone and timbered with local oak. "It is as if the mountain offered itself as a dwelling place for spiritual practice" is how the monks of the monastery describe it in their official literature. Pushing past the oaken double doors, Thomas was greeted by a monk who had been tasked with welcoming newcomers. Struggling to describe the emotions of this experience, Thomas finally managed to explain it to me as follows: "It was like being really hungry, and you know that you're going to get this amazing meal—that is what this represented for me."

Thomas's new life as a monk started well enough. He lived in a small cabin, set back in the woods from the main building. Early in his visit he asked a senior monk, who had been living in a similar cabin for over fifteen years, if he ever got tired of walking the trail connecting the residences to the main building. "I'm only just starting to learn it," the monk replied mindfully.

The days at the Zen Mountain Monastery started as early as 4:30 A.M., depending on the time of year. Remaining in silence, the monks would greet the morning with forty to eighty minutes of meditation on mats arranged with "geometric precision" in the main hall. The view outside the Gothic windows at the front of the hall was spectacular, but the mats kept the meditators too low to see out. A pair of hall monitors sat at the back of the room, occasionally pacing among the mats. Thomas explained: "If you found yourself falling asleep, you could request that they hit you with a stick they kept for this purpose."

After breakfast, eaten in the same great hall, everyone was assigned jobs. Thomas spent time cleaning toilets and shoveling ditches as part of his housecleaning duties, but he was also assigned, somewhat anachronistically, to handle the graphic design for the monastery's print journal. A typical day continued with more meditation, interviews with senior practitioners, and often long, inscrutable Dharma lectures. The monks were given a break each evening before dinner. Thomas often took advantage of this respite to light the woodstove in his cabin, preparing for the cold Catskill nights.

Thomas's problems began with the koans. A koan, in the Zen tradition, is a word puzzle, often presented as a story or a question. They're meant to defy logical answers and therefore force you to access a more intuitive understanding of reality. In explaining the concept to me, Thomas gave the following example, which he had encountered early in his practice: "Show me an immovable tree in a heavy wind."

"I don't even know what an answer to that would look like," I protested.

"In an interview," he explained, "you have to answer right away, no thinking. If you pause like that, they kick you out of the room; the interview is over."

"Okay, I would have been kicked out."

"Here's the answer I gave to pass the koan," he said. "I stood, like a tree, and waved my hands slightly as if in a wind. Right? The point was that this is a concept you really couldn't capture in words."

One of the first major hurdles a young practitioner faces in serious Zen practice is the Mu koan: Passing this koan is the first of the "eight gates" of Zen Buddhism. Until you reach this milestone, you're not yet considered a serious student of the practice. Thomas seemed reluctant to explain this koan to me. I had encountered this before in my research on Zen: Because these puzzles defy rationality, any attempt to describe them to a non-practitioner can be trivializing. Because of this I didn't press Thomas for details. Instead, I Googled it. Here's one translation I found:

A pilgrim of the way asked the Grand Master Zhaozhou, "Does a dog have Buddha nature or not?" Zhaozhou said, "Mu."

In Chinese, *mu* translates roughly to "no." According to the interpretations I found, Zhaozhou is not answering the pilgrim's question, but is instead pushing it back to the questioner. Thomas struggled to pass this koan, focusing on it intensely for months. "I worked and worked on that koan," he told me. "I went to bed with it; I let it inhabit my whole body."

Then he cracked it.

"One day I was walking in the forest, and a moment passed. I had been looking at these leaves, and 'I' had disappeared. We all experience things like this but don't attach any importance to them. But when I had this experience, I was prepared for it, and it clicked. I realized, 'This is the whole koan.'" Thomas had achieved a glimpse of the unity of nature that forms the core of the Buddhist understanding of the world. It was this unity that provided the answer to the koan. Excited, at his next interview with a senior monk Thomas made a gesture—"a simple gesture, something you might do in everyday life"—that made it clear that he had an intuitive understanding of the koan's answer. He had made it through the first gate: He was officially a serious student of Zen.

It was not long after passing the Mu koan that Thomas had his realization about passion. He was walking in the same woods where he had cracked the koan. Armed with the insight provided by passing the Mu, he had begun to understand the once obtuse lectures given most days by the senior monks. "As I walked that trail, I realized that these lectures were all talking about the same thing as the Mu koan," said Thomas. In other words, *this was it. This was what life as a Zen monk offered*: increasingly sophisticated musings on this one, core insight.

He had reached the zenith of his passion—he could

now properly call himself a Zen practitioner—*and yet*, he was not experiencing the undiluted peace and happiness that had populated his daydreams.

"The reality was, nothing had changed. I was exactly the same person, with the same worries and anxieties. It was late on a Sunday afternoon when I came to this realization, and I just started crying."

Thomas had followed his passion to the Zen Mountain Monastery, believing, as many do, that the key to happiness is identifying your true calling and then chasing after it with all the courage you can muster. But as Thomas experienced that late Sunday afternoon in the oak forest, this belief is frighteningly naïve. Fulfilling his dream to become a full-time Zen practitioner did *not* magically make his life wonderful.

As Thomas discovered, the path to happiness—at least as it concerns what you do for a living—is more complicated than simply answering the classic question *"What should I do with my life?"*

A Quest Begins

By the summer of 2010, I had become obsessed with answering a simple question: *Why do some people end up loving what they do, while so many others fail at this goal?* It was this obsession that led me to people like Thomas, whose stories helped cement an insight I had long suspected to be true: When it comes to creating work you love, following your passion is not particularly useful advice.

The explanation for what started me down this path goes something like this: During the summer of 2010, when this preoccupation first picked up steam, I was a postdoctoral associate at MIT, where I had earned my PhD in computer science the year before. I was on track to become a professor, which, at a graduate program like MIT's, is considered to be the only respectable path. If done right, a professorship is a job for life. In other words, in 2010 I was planning what might well be my first and last job hunt. If there was ever a time to figure out what generates a passion for one's livelihood, this was it.

Tugging more insistently at my attention during this period was the very real possibility that I wouldn't end up with a professorship at all. Not long after meeting Thomas, I had set up a meeting with my advisor to discuss my academic job search. "How bad of a school are you willing to go to?" was his opening question. The academic job market is always brutal, but in 2010, with an economy still in recession, it was especially tough.

To complicate matters, my research specialty hadn't proven to be all that popular in recent years. The last two students to graduate from the group where I wrote my dissertation both ended up with professorships in Asia, while the last two postdocs to pass through the group ended up in Lugano, Switzerland, and Winnipeg,

Canada, respectively. "I have to say, I found the whole process to be pretty hard, stressful, and depressing," one of these former students told me. Given that my wife and I wanted to stay in the United States, and preferably on the East Coast, a choice that drastically narrowed our options, I had to face the very real possibility that my academic job search would be a bust, forcing me to essentially start from scratch in figuring out what to do with my life.

This was the backdrop against which I launched what I eventually began to refer to as "my quest." My question was clear: *How do people end up loving what they do?* And I needed an answer.

This book documents what I discovered in my search.

———————

Here's what you can expect in the pages ahead:

As mentioned, I didn't get far in my quest before I realized, as Thomas did before me, that the conventional wisdom on career success—*follow your passion*—is seriously flawed. It not only fails to describe how most people actually end up with compelling careers, but for many people it can actually make things worse: leading to chronic job shifting and unrelenting angst when, as it did for Thomas, one's reality inevitably falls short of the dream.

With this as a starting point, I begin with Rule #1, in which I tear down the supremacy of this *passion hypothesis.* But I don't stop there. My quest pushed me beyond identifying what doesn't work, insisting that I also answer the following: **If "follow your passion" is bad advice, what should I do instead?** My search for this answer, described in Rules #2–4, brought me to unexpected places. To better understand the importance of autonomy, for example, I ended up spending a day at an organic farm owned by a young Ivy League graduate. To better nuance my understanding of skill, I spent time with professional musicians—examples of a dying craftsman culture that I thought had something important to say about how we approach work. I also dived into the world of venture capitalists, screenwriters, rock-star computer programmers, and of course, hotshot professors, to name just a few more examples among many—all in an effort to pick apart what matters and what doesn't when building a compelling career. I was surprised by how many sources of insight became visible once I burned off the obscuring fog generated by a mono-focused insistence on following your passion.

The narratives in this book are bound by a common thread: *the importance of ability.* The things that make a great job great, I discovered, are rare and valuable. If you want them in your working life, you need something rare and valuable to offer in return. In other words, you need to be good at something before you can expect a good job.

Of course, mastery by itself is not enough to guarantee happiness: The many examples of well-respected but miserable workaholics support this claim. Accordingly, this main thread of my argument moves beyond the mere acquisition of useful skills and into the subtle art of investing the *career capital* this generates into the right types of traits in your working life.

This argument flips conventional wisdom. It relegates passion to the sidelines, claiming that this feeling is an epiphenomenon of a working life well lived. Don't follow your passion; rather, let it follow *you* in your quest to become, in the words of my favorite Steve Martin quote, "so good that they can't ignore you."

To many, this concept is a radical shift, and as with any disruptive idea, it needs to make a splashy entrance. This is why I wrote this book in a manifesto style. I divided the content into four "rules," each given a deliberately provocative title. I also tried to make the book short and punchy: I want to introduce a new way of looking at the world, but I don't want to belabor the insights with excessive examples and discussions. This book *does* offer concrete advice, but you won't find ten-step systems or self-assessment quizzes in these pages. This topic is too subtle to be reduced to the formulaic.

By the end of this book, you'll have learned how my own story ends up and the specific ways I'm applying the insights in my own working life. We'll also return to Thomas, who after his dispiriting realization at the monastery was able to return to his first principles, move his focus away from finding the *right work* and toward *working right,* and eventually build, for the first time in his life, a love for what he does. This is the happiness that you, too, should demand.

It's my hope that the insights that follow will free you from simplistic catchphrases like "follow your passion" and "do what you love"—the type of catchphrases that have helped spawn the career confusion that afflicts so many today—and instead, provide you with a *realistic* path toward a meaningful and engaging working life.

RULE #1

Don't Follow Your Passion

Chapter One

The "Passion" of Steve Jobs

*In which I question the validity of **the passion hypothesis**, which says that the key to occupational happiness is to match your job to a pre-existing passion.*

The Passion Hypothesis

In June 2005, Steve Jobs took the podium at Stanford Stadium to give the commencement speech to Stanford's graduating class. Wearing jeans and sandals under his formal robe, Jobs addressed a crowd of 23,000 with a short speech that drew lessons from his life. About a third of the way into the address, Jobs offered the following advice:

> *You've got to find what you love.... [T]he only way to do great work is to love what you do. If you haven't found it yet, keep looking, and don't settle.*

When he finished, he received a standing ovation.

Though Jobs's address contained several different lessons, his emphasis on doing what you love was the clear standout. In the official press release describing the event, for example, Stanford's news service reported that Jobs "urged graduates to pursue their dreams."

Soon after, an unofficial video of the address was posted on YouTube, where it went viral, gathering over 3.5 million views. When Stanford posted an official video, it gathered an additional 3 million views. The comments on these clips homed in on the importance of loving your work, with viewers summarizing their reactions in similar ways:

"The most valuable lesson is to find your purpose, follow your passions. . . . Life is too short to be doing what you think you have to do."

"Follow your passions—life is for the living."

"Passion is the engine to living your life."

"[It's] passion for your work that counts."

" 'Don't Settle.' Amen."

In other words, many of the millions of people who viewed this speech were excited to see Steve Jobs—a guru of iconoclastic thinking—put his stamp of approval on an immensely appealing piece of popular career advice, which I call the passion hypothesis:

The Passion Hypothesis

The key to occupational happiness is to first figure out what you're passionate about and then find a job that matches this passion.

This hypothesis is one of modern American society's most well-worn themes. Those of us lucky enough to have some choice in what we do with our lives are bombarded with this message, starting at an early age. We are told to lionize those with the courage to follow their passion, and pity the conformist drones who cling to the safe path.

If you doubt the ubiquity of this message, spend a few minutes browsing the career-advice shelf the next time you visit a bookstore. Once you look past the technical manuals on résumé writing and job-interview etiquette, it's hard to find a book that doesn't promote the passion hypothesis. These books have titles like *Career Match: Connecting Who You Are with What You'll Love to Do*, and *Do What You Are: Discover the Perfect Career for You Through the Secrets of Personality Type*, and they promise that you're just a few personality tests away from finding your dream job. Recently, a new, more aggressive strain of the passion hypothesis has been spreading—a strain that despairs that traditional "cubicle jobs," by their very nature, are bad, and that passion requires that you strike out on your own. This is where you find titles like *Escape from Cubicle Nation*, which, as one review described it, "teaches the tricks behind finding what makes you purr."

These books, as well as the thousands of full-time bloggers, professional counselors, and self-proclaimed gurus who orbit these same core issues of workplace happiness, all peddle the same lesson: *to be happy, you must follow your passion.* As one prominent career counselor told me, "do what you love, and the money will follow" has become the de facto motto of the career-advice field.

There is, however, a problem lurking here: When you look past the feel-good slogans and go deeper into the details of how passionate people like Steve Jobs really got started, or ask scientists about what actually predicts workplace happiness, the issue becomes much more complicated. You begin to find threads of nuance that, once pulled, unravel the tight certainty of the passion hypothesis, eventually leading to an unsettling recognition: **"Follow your passion" might just be terrible advice.**

It was around the time I was transitioning from graduate school that I started to pull on these threads, eventually leading to my complete rejection of the passion hypothesis and kicking off my quest to find out what really matters for creating work you love. Rule #1 is dedicated to laying out my argument against passion, as this insight— that "follow your passion" is bad advice—provides the foundation for everything that follows. Perhaps the best place to start is where we began, with the real story of Steve Jobs and the founding of Apple Computer.

Do What Steve Jobs Did, Not What He Said

If you had met a young Steve Jobs in the years leading up to his founding of Apple Computer, you wouldn't have pegged him as someone who was passionate about starting a technology company. Jobs had attended Reed College, a prestigious liberal arts enclave in Oregon, where he grew his hair long and took to walking barefoot. Unlike other technology visionaries of his era, Jobs wasn't particularly interested in either business or electronics as a student. He instead studied Western history and dance, and dabbled in Eastern mysticism.

Jobs dropped out of college after his first year, but remained on campus for a while, sleeping on floors and scrounging free meals at the local Hare Krishna temple. His non-conformity made him a campus celebrity— a "freak" in the terminology of the times. As Jeffrey S. Young notes in his exhaustively researched 1988 biography, *Steve Jobs: The Journey Is the Reward*, Jobs eventually grew tired of being a pauper and, during the early 1970s, returned home to California, where he moved back in with his parents and talked himself into a nightshift job at Atari. (The company had caught his attention with an ad in the *San Jose Mercury News* that read, "Have fun and make money.") During this period, Jobs split his time between Atari and the All-One Farm, a country commune located north of San Francisco. At one point, he left his job at Atari for several months to make a mendicants' spiritual journey through India, and on returning home he began to train seriously at the nearby Los Altos Zen Center.

In 1974, after Jobs's return from India, a local

engineer and entrepreneur named Alex Kamradt started a computer time-sharing company dubbed Call-in Computer. Kamradt approached Steve Wozniak to design a terminal device he could sell to clients to use for accessing his central computer. Unlike Jobs, Wozniak was a true electronics whiz who was obsessed with technology and had studied it formally at college. On the flip side, however, Wozniak couldn't stomach business, so he allowed Jobs, a longtime friend, to handle the details of the arrangement. All was going well until the fall of 1975, when Jobs left for the season to spend time at the All-One commune. Unfortunately, he failed to tell Kamradt he was leaving. When he returned, he had been replaced.

I tell this story because these are hardly the actions of someone passionate about technology and entrepreneurship, yet this was less than a year before Jobs started Apple Computer. In other words, in the months leading up to the start of his visionary company, Steve Jobs was something of a conflicted young man, seeking spiritual enlightenment and dabbling in electronics only when it promised to earn him quick cash.

It was with this mindset that later that same year, Jobs stumbled into his big break. He noticed that the local "wireheads" were excited by the introduction of model-kit computers that enthusiasts could assemble at home. (He wasn't alone in noticing the potential of this excitement. When an ambitious young Harvard student saw the first kit computer grace the cover of *Popular Electronics* magazine, he formed a company to develop a version of the BASIC programming language for the new machine, eventually dropping out of school to grow the business. He called the new firm Microsoft.)

Jobs pitched Wozniak the idea of designing one of these kit computer circuit boards so they could sell them to local hobbyists. The initial plan was to make the boards for $25 apiece and sell them for $50. Jobs wanted to sell one hundred, total, which, after removing the costs of printing the boards, and a $1,500 fee for the initial board design, would leave them with a nice $1,000 profit. Neither Wozniak nor Jobs left their regular jobs: This was strictly a low-risk venture meant for their free time.

From this point, however, the story quickly veers into legend. Steve arrived barefoot at the Byte Shop, Paul Terrell's pioneering Mountain View computer store, and offered Terrell the circuit boards for sale. Terrell didn't want to sell plain boards, but said he would buy fully assembled computers. He would pay $500 for each, and wanted fifty as soon as they could be delivered. Jobs jumped at the opportunity to make an even larger amount of money and began scrounging together start-up capital. It was in this unexpected windfall that Apple Computer was born. As Young emphasizes, "Their plans were circumspect and small-time. They weren't dreaming of taking over the world."

The Messy Lessons of Jobs

I shared the details of Steve Jobs's story, because when it comes to finding fulfilling work, the details matter. If a young Steve Jobs had taken his own advice and decided to only pursue work he loved, we would probably find him today as one of the Los Altos Zen Center's most popular teachers. But he didn't follow this simple advice. Apple Computer was decidedly not born out of passion, but instead was the result of a lucky break—a "small-time" scheme that unexpectedly took off.

I don't doubt that Jobs eventually grew passionate about his work: If you've watched one of his famous keynote addresses, you've seen a man who obviously loved what he did. *But so what?* All that tells us is that *it's good to enjoy what you do.* This advice, though true, borders on the tautological and doesn't help us with the pressing question that we actually care about: *How do we find work that we'll eventually love?* Like Jobs, should we resist settling into one rigid career and instead try lots of small schemes, waiting for one to take off? Does it matter what general field we explore? How do we know when to stick with a project or when to move on? In other words, Jobs's story generates more questions than it answers. Perhaps the only thing it does make clear is that, at least for Jobs, "follow your passion" was not particularly useful advice.

Chapter Two

Passion Is Rare

In which I argue that the more you seek examples of the passion hypothesis, the more you recognize its rarity.

The *Roadtrip Nation* Revelation

It turns out that Jobs's complicated path to fulfilling work is common among interesting people with interesting careers. In 2001, a group of four friends, all recently graduated from college, set out on a cross-country road trip to interview people who "[lived] lives centered around what was meaningful to them." The friends sought advice for shaping their own careers into something fulfilling. They filmed a documentary about their trip, which was then expanded into a series on PBS. They eventually launched a nonprofit called Roadtrip Nation, with the goal of helping other young people replicate their journey. What makes Roadtrip Nation relevant is that it maintains an extensive video library of the interviews conducted for the project.[1] There's perhaps no better single resource for diving into the reality of how people end up with compelling careers.

When you spend time with this archive, which is available for free online, you soon notice that the messy nature of Steve Jobs's path is more the rule than the exception. In an interview with the public radio host Ira Glass, for example, a group of three undergraduates press him for wisdom on how to "figure out what you want" and "know what you'll be good at."

"In the movies there's this idea that you should just go for your dream," Glass tells them. "But I don't believe that. Things happen in stages."

Glass emphasizes that it takes time to get good at anything, recounting the many years it took him to master radio to the point where he had interesting options. "The key thing is to force yourself through the work, force the skills to come; that's the hardest phase," he says.

Noticing the stricken faces of his interviewers, who were perhaps hoping to hear something more uplifting than *work is hard, so suck it up,* Glass continues: "I feel like your problem is that you're trying to judge all things in the abstract before you do them. That's your tragic mistake."[2]

Other interviews in the archive promote this same idea that it's hard to predict in advance what you'll eventually grow to love. The astrobiologist Andrew Steele, for example, exclaims, "No, I had no idea what I was going to do. I object to systems that say you should decide now what you're going to do." One of the students asks Steele if he had started his PhD program "hoping you'd one day change the world."

"No," Steele responds, "I just wanted options."[3]

Al Merrick, the founder of Channel Island Surfboards, tells a similar tale of stumbling into passion over time. "People are in a rush to start their lives, and it's sad," he tells his interviewers. "I didn't go out with the idea of making a big empire," he explains. "I set goals for myself at being the best I could be at what[ever] I did."[4]

In another clip, William Morris, a renowned glass blower based in Stanwood, Washington, brings a group of students to his workshop set in a converted barn surrounded by lush, Pacific Northwest forest. "I have a ton of different interests, and I don't have focus," one of the students complains. Morris looks at her: "You'll never be sure. You don't want to be sure."[5]

These interviews emphasize an important point: **Compelling careers often have complex origins that reject the simple idea that all you have to do is follow your passion.**

This observation may come as a surprise for those of us who have long basked in the glow of the passion hypothesis. It wouldn't, however, surprise the many scientists who have studied questions of workplace satisfaction using rigorous peer-reviewed research. They've been discovering similar conclusions for decades, but to date, not many people in the career-advice field have paid them serious attention. It's to these overlooked research efforts that I turn your attention next.

The Science of Passion

Why do some people enjoy their work while so many other people don't? Here's the CliffsNotes summary of the social science research in this area: There are many complex reasons for workplace satisfaction, but the reductive notion of matching your job to a pre-existing passion is not among them.

To give you a better sense of the realities uncovered by this research, here are three of the more interesting conclusions I've encountered:

Conclusion #1: Career Passions Are Rare

In 2002, a research team led by the Canadian psychologist Robert J. Vallerand administered an extensive questionnaire to a group of 539 Canadian university students.[6] The questionnaire's prompts were designed to answer two important questions: *Do these students have passions? And if so, what are they?*

At the core of the passion hypothesis is the assumption that we all have pre-existing passions waiting to be discovered. This experiment puts that assumption to the test. Here's what it found: 84 percent of the students surveyed were identified as having a passion. This sounds like good news for supporters of the passion hypothesis—that is, until you dive deeper into the details of these pursuits. Here are the top five identified passions: dance, hockey (these were Canadian students, mind you), skiing, reading, and swimming. Though dear to the hearts of the students, these passions don't have much to offer when it comes to choosing a job. In fact, less than 4 percent of the total identified passions had *any* relation to work or education, with the remaining 96 percent describing hobby-style interests such as sports and art.

Take a moment to absorb this result, as it deals a strong blow to the passion hypothesis. How can we follow our passions if we don't have any relevant passions to follow? At least for these Canadian college students, the vast majority will need a different strategy for choosing their career.

Conclusion #2: Passion Takes Time

Amy Wrzesniewski, a professor of organizational behavior at Yale University, has made a career studying how people think about their work. Her breakthrough paper, published in the *Journal of Research in Personality* while she was still a graduate student, explores the distinction between a job, a career, and a calling.[7] A *job*, in Wrzesniewski's formulation, is a way to pay the bills, a *career* is a path toward increasingly better work, and a *calling* is work that's an important part of your life and a vital part of your identity.

Wrzesniewski surveyed employees from a variety of occupations, from doctors to computer programmers to clerical workers, and found that most people strongly identify their work with one of these three categories. A possible explanation for these different classifications is that some occupations are better than others. The passion hypothesis, for example, predicts that occupations that match common passions, such as being a doctor or a teacher, should have a high proportion of people who experience the work as a true calling, while less flashy occupations—the type that no one daydreams about—should have almost no one experiencing the work as a calling. To test this explanation, Wrzesniewski looked at a group of employees who all had the *same* position and nearly identical work responsibilities: college administrative assistants. She found, to her admitted surprise, that these employees were roughly evenly split between seeing their position as a job, a career, or a calling. In other words, it seems that the type of work alone does not necessarily predict how much people enjoy it.

Supporters of the passion hypothesis, however, might reply that a position like a college administrative assistant will attract a wide variety of employees. Some might arrive at the position because they have a passion for higher education and will therefore love the work, while others might stumble into the job for other reasons, perhaps because it's stable and has good benefits, and therefore will have a less exalted experience.

But Wrzesniewski wasn't done. She surveyed the assistants to figure out *why* they saw their work so differently, and discovered that the strongest predictor of an assistant seeing her work as a calling was the number of years spent on the job. In other words, the more experience an assistant had, the more likely she was to love her work.

This result deals another blow to the passion hypothesis. In Wrzesniewski's research, the happiest, most passionate employees are not those who followed their passion into a position, but instead those who have been around long enough to become good at what they do. On reflection, this makes sense. If you have many years' experience, then you've had time to get better at what you do and develop a feeling of efficacy. It also gives you time to develop strong relationships with your coworkers and to see many examples of your work benefiting others. What's important here, however, is that this explanation, though reasonable, contradicts the passion hypothesis, which instead emphasizes the immediate happiness that comes from matching your job to a true passion.

Conclusion #3: Passion Is a Side Effect of Mastery

Not long into his popular TED talk, titled "On the Surprising Science of Motivation," author Daniel Pink, discussing his book *Drive*, tells the audience that he spent the last couple of years studying the science of human motivation. "I'm telling you, it's not even close," he says. "If you look at the science, there is a mismatch between what science knows and what business does." When

Pink talks about "what science knows," he's referring, for the most part, to a forty-year-old theoretical framework known as Self-Determination Theory (SDT), which is arguably the best understanding science currently has for why some pursuits get our engines running while others leave us cold.[8]

SDT tells us that motivation, in the workplace or elsewhere, requires that you fulfill three basic psychological needs—factors described as the "nutriments" required to feel intrinsically motivated for your work:

- **Autonomy**: the feeling that you have control over your day, and that your actions are important
- **Competence**: the feeling that you are good at what you do
- **Relatedness**: the feeling of connection to other people

The last need is the least surprising: If you feel close to people at work, you're going to enjoy work more. It's the first two needs that prove more interesting. It's clear, for example, that autonomy and competence are related. In most jobs, as you become better at what you do, not only do you get the sense of accomplishment that comes from being good, but you're typically also rewarded with more control over your responsibilities. These results help explain Amy Wrzesniewski's findings: Perhaps one reason that more experienced assistants enjoyed their work was because it takes time to build the competence and autonomy that generates this enjoyment.

Of equal interest is what this list of basic psychological needs does *not* include. Notice, scientists did not find "matching work to pre-existing passions" as being important for motivation. The traits they *did* find, by contrast, are more general and are agnostic to the specific type of work in question. Competence and autonomy, for example, are achievable by most people in a wide variety of jobs—assuming they're willing to put in the hard work required for mastery. This message is not as inspiring as "follow your passion and you'll immediately be happy," but it certainly has a ring of truth. In other words, working right trumps finding the right work.

Chapter Three

Passion Is Dangerous

In which I argue that subscribing to the passion hypothesis can make you less happy.

The Birth of the Passion Hypothesis

It's difficult to pinpoint the exact moment when our society began emphasizing the importance of following your passion, but a good approximation is the 1970 publication of *What Color Is Your Parachute?* The author, Richard Bolles, was working at the time for the Episcopal Church advising campus ministers, many of whom were in danger of losing their jobs. He published the first edition of *Parachute* as a straightforward collection of tips for those facing career change. The original print run was one hundred copies.

The premise of Bolles's guide sounds self-evident to the modern ear: "[Figure] out what you like to do...and then find a place that needs people like you." But in 1970, this was a radical notion. "[At the time,] the idea of doing a lot of pen-and-paper exercises in order to take control of your own career was regarded as a dilettante's exercise," Bolles recalls.[1] The optimism of this message, however, caught on: *You* can control what you do with your life, so why not pursue what you love? There are now more than six million copies of Bolles's book in print.

The decades since the publication of Bolles's book can be understood as a period of increasing dedication to the passion hypothesis. You can visualize this shift by using Google's Ngram Viewer.[2] This tool allows you to search Google's vast corpus of digitized books to see how often selected phrases turn up in published writing over time. If you enter "follow your passion," you see a spike in usage right at 1970 (the year when Bolles's book was published), followed by a relatively steady high usage until 1990, at which point the graph curve swings upward. By 2000, the phrase "follow your passion" was showing up in print three times more often than in the seventies and eighties.

Parachute, in other words, helped introduce the baby boom generation to this passion-centric take on career, a lesson they have now passed down to their children, the echo boom generation, which has since raised the bar on passion obsession. This young generation has "high expectations for work," explains psychologist Jeffrey Arnett, an expert on the mindset of the modern postgrad. "They expect work to be not just a job but an adventure[,]...a venue for self-development and self-expression[,]...and something that provides a satisfying fit with their assessment of their talents."[3]

Even if you accept my argument that the passion hypothesis is flawed, it's at this point that you might respond, "Who cares!" If the passion hypothesis can encourage even a small number of people to leave a bad job or to experiment with their career, you might argue, then it has provided a service. The fact that this occupational fairy tale has spread so far should not cause concern.

I disagree. The more I studied the issue, the more I noticed that the passion hypothesis convinces people that somewhere there's a magic "right" job waiting for them, and that if they find it, they'll immediately recognize that this is the work *they were meant to do.* The problem, of course, is when they fail to find this certainty, bad things follow, such as chronic job-hopping and crippling self-doubt.

We can see this effect in the statistics. As I just established, the last several decades are marked by an increasing commitment to Bolles's contagious idea. And yet, for all of this increased focus on following our passion and holding out for work we love, *we aren't getting any happier.* The 2010 Conference Board survey of U.S. job satisfaction found that only 45 percent of Americans describe themselves as satisfied with their jobs. This number has been steadily decreasing from the mark of 61 percent recorded in 1987, the first year of the survey. As Lynn Franco, the director of the Board's Consumer Research Center notes, this is not just about a bad business cycle: "Through both economic boom and bust during the past two decades, our job satisfaction numbers have shown a consistent downward trend." Among young people, the group perhaps most concerned with the role of work in their lives, 64 percent now say that they're actively unhappy in their jobs. This is the highest level of dissatisfaction ever measured for any age group over the full two-decade history of the survey.[4] In other words, our generation-spanning experiment with passion-centric career planning can be deemed a failure: The more we focused on loving what we do, the less we ended up loving it.

These statistics, of course, are not clear-cut, as other factors play a role in declining workplace happiness. To develop a more visceral understanding of this unease, we can turn to anecdotal sources. Consider Alexandra Robbins and Abby Wilner's 2001 ode to youth disaffection, *Quarterlife Crisis: The Unique Challenges of Life in Your Twenties*. This book chronicles the personal testimony of dozens of unhappy twentysomethings who feel adrift in the world of work. Take, for example, the tale of Scott, a twenty-seven-year-old from Washington, D.C.

"My professional situation now couldn't be more perfect," Scott reports. "I chose to pursue the career I knew in my heart I was passionate about: politics....I love my office, my friends...even my boss." The glamorous promises of the passion hypothesis, however, led Scott to question whether his perfect job was perfect enough. "It's not fulfilling," he worries when reflecting on the fact that his job, like all jobs, includes difficult responsibilities. He has since restarted his search for his life's work. "I've committed myself to exploring other options that interest me," Scott says. "But I'm having a hard time actually thinking of a career that sounds appealing."

"I graduated college wanting nothing more than the ultimate job for me," says Jill, another young person profiled in *Quarterlife Crisis*. Not surprisingly, everything Jill tried failed to meet this high mark.

"I'm so lost about what I want to do," despairs twenty-five-year-old Elaine, "that I don't even realize what I'm sacrificing."[5]

And so on. These stories, which are increasingly common at all ages, from college students to the middle-aged, all point toward the same conclusion: **The passion hypothesis is not just wrong, it's also dangerous.** Telling someone to "follow their passion" is not just an act of innocent optimism, but potentially the foundation for a career riddled with confusion and angst.

Beyond Passion

Before continuing, I should emphasize an obvious point: For some people, following their passion works. The Roadtrip Nation archives, for example, include an interview with *Rolling Stone* film critic Peter Travers, who claims that even as a child he used to bring notebooks into movie theaters to record his thoughts.[6] The power of passion is even more common when you look to the careers of gifted individuals, such as professional athletes. You'd be hard-pressed, for example, to find a professional baseball player who doesn't claim that he has been passionate about the sport as far back as he can remember.

Some people I've talked to about my ideas have used examples of this type to dismiss my conclusions about passion. "Here's a case where someone successfully followed their passion," they say, "therefore 'follow your passion' must be good advice." This is faulty logic. Observing a few instances of a strategy working does not make it universally effective. It is necessary instead to study a large number of examples and ask what worked in the vast majority of the cases. And when you study a large group of people who are passionate about what they do, as I did in researching this book, you find that most—*not all*—will tell a story more complex than simply identifying a pre-existing passion and then pursuing it. Examples such as Peter Travers and professional athletes, therefore, are exceptions. If anything, their rareness underscores my claim that for *most people*, "follow your passion" is bad advice.

This conclusion inspires an important follow-up question: Without the passion hypothesis to guide us, what should we do instead? This is the question I take up in the three rules that follow. These rules chronicle my quest to figure out how people *really* end up loving what they do. They represent a shift away from the tone of lawyerly argument used here and into something more personal: evidence of my attempts to capture the complexity and ambiguity of my encounters with the reality of workplace happiness. With the thorny underbrush of the passion hypothesis cleared, we can only now bring light to a more realistic strain of career advice that has so long been strangled in the shadows. This is a process that begins in the next rule with my arrival at an unlikely source of insight: a group of bluegrass musicians practicing their craft in the suburbs of Boston.

Be So Good They Can't Ignore You

(Or, *the Importance of Skill*)

Chapter Four

The Clarity of the Craftsman

*In which I introduce two different approaches to thinking about work: **the craftsman mindset**, a focus on what value you're producing in your job, and **the passion mindset**, a focus on what value your job offers you. Most people adopt the passion mindset, but in this chapter I argue that the craftsman mindset is the foundation for creating work you love.*

Upstairs at the Bluegrass Frat House

When I first rounded the corner onto Mapleton Street, the house, a careworn Victorian, blended in with its tidy suburban neighbors. It was only as I got closer that I noticed the eccentricities. The paint was peeling. There was a pair of leather recliners outside on the porch. Empty Bud Light bottles littered the ground.

Jordan Tice, a professional guitar player of the New Acoustic style, stood by the front door smoking a cigarette. He waved me over. As I followed him inside, I noticed that a small foyer set off the entry had been converted into a bedroom. "The banjo player who sleeps there has a PhD from MIT," Jordan said. "You'd like him."

Jordan is one of many musicians who come and go from the rental, squeezing themselves into any space that meets the technical definition of habitable. "Welcome to the bluegrass frat house," he said, by way of explanation as we headed up to the second floor where he lives. Jordan's room is monastic. Smaller than any dorm room I had at college, it's just big enough for a twin bed and a simple pressboard desk. A Fender tube amp sits in one corner and a rolling luggage bag in the other. Most of his guitars, I assume, are kept downstairs in the common practice space, as I only saw one in the room, a beat-up Martin. We had to borrow a chair from another room so that we could both sit.

Jordan is twenty-four. In the world of traditional work this is young, but when you consider that he signed his first record deal while still in high school, it's clear that in the world of acoustic music Jordan's no rookie. He's also painfully modest. One review of his third album, *Long Story*, began, "Music has always had its share of prodigies, from Mozart up to the current day."[1] This is exactly the type of praise that Jordan would hate for me to write about. When I asked him why Gary Ferguson, a well-known bluegrass artist, chose Jordan at the age of sixteen to tour with him, he could only stammer, before lapsing into silence.

"It's a big deal," I pushed. "He chose you to be his guitar player. He had his choice of lots of guitar players, and he chose a sixteen-year-old."

"I don't derive any arrogance from that specific thing," he finally answered.

Here's what does excite Jordan: his music. When I asked him, "What are you working on today?" his eyes lit up as he grabbed an open composition book from his desk. On it were five lines of music, lightly penciled in—mainly dense runs of quarter notes spanning up and down the octave, punctuated with the occasional handwritten explanation. "I'm kinda working on a new tune," he explained. "It's going to be really fast."

Jordan picked up his Martin to play me the new song. It had the driving beat of bluegrass, but the melody, which was inspired by a Debussy composition, happily disregards the genre. When Jordan played, he stared just beyond the fretboard and breathed in sharp, sporadic gasps. At one point he missed a note, which upset him. He backed up and started again, insisting on playing until he finished the full phrase without mistake.

I told him I was impressed by the speed of the licks. "No, this is slow," he replied. He then showed me the pace he's working toward: It's at least twice as fast. "I can't quite make the lead trail yet," he apologized after it slipped away from him. "I guess I *could* do it, but I can't get the notes to pop out yet like I want it." He showed me how the successive notes in the lead tend to span many strings, complicating fast picking. "It's really wide."

At my request, Jordan laid out his practice regimen for this song. He starts by playing slow enough that he can get the effects he desires: He wants the key notes of the melody to ring while he fills the space in between with runs up and down the fretboard. Then he adds speed—just enough that he can't quite make things work. He repeats this again and again. "It's a physical and mental exercise," he explained. "You're trying to keep track of different melodies and things. In a piano, everything is laid out clearly in front of you; ten fingers never getting in the way of one another. On the guitar, you have to budget your fingers."

He called his work on this song his "technical focus" of the moment. In a typical day, if he's not preparing for a show, he'll practice with this same intensity, always playing just a little faster than he's comfortable, for two or three hours straight. I asked him how long it will take to finally master the new skill. "Probably like a month," he guessed. Then he played through the lick one more time.

The Craftsman Mindset

Let me be clear about something: I really don't care if Jordan Tice loves what he does. I also don't care why he decided to become a musician or whether he sees guitar playing as his "passion." Musicians' career paths are idiosyncratic, often relying on unusual circumstances and lucky breaks early in life. (The fact that Jordan's parents are both bluegrass musicians, for example, obviously played a big role in his early dedication to guitar.)

Because of this, I've never found the origin stories of performers' careers to be all that relevant to the rest of us. Here's what *does* interest me about Jordan: how he approaches his work on a daily basis. Lurking here, I · discovered, is an insight of great value to my quest for work I love.

The path that led me to Jordan and the insight he represents began with a 2007 episode of the *Charlie Rose* show. Rose was interviewing the actor and comedian Steve Martin about his memoir *Born Standing Up.*[2] They talked about the realities of Martin's rise. "I read autobiographies in general," Martin said. "[And I often get frustrated]...and say, 'You left out that one part here, how did you get that audition for that one thing where suddenly you're working at the Copa? How did that happen?'" Martin wrote his book to answer the "how" question, at least with respect to his own success in stand-up. It was in this explanation of "how" that Martin introduced a simple idea that floored me when I first heard it. The quote comes in the last five minutes of the interview, when Rose asks Martin his advice for aspiring performers.

"Nobody ever takes note of [my advice], because it's not the answer they wanted to hear," Martin said. "What they want to hear is 'Here's how you get an agent, here's how you write a script,'...but I always say, **'Be so good · they can't ignore you.'"**

In response to Rose's trademark ambiguous grunt,

Martin defended his advice: "If somebody's thinking, 'How can I be really good?' people are going to come to you."

This is exactly the philosophy that catapulted Martin into stardom. He was only twenty years old when he decided to innovate his act into something too good to be ignored. "Comedy at the time was all setup and punch line...the clichéd nightclub comedian, rat-a-tat-tat," Martin explained to Rose.[3] He thought it could be something more sophisticated. Here's how Martin explained his evolution in an article he published around the time of his Charlie Rose interview: "What if there were no punch lines? What if there were no indicators? What if I created tension and never released it? What if I headed for a climax, but all I delivered was an anticlimax?"[4] In one famous bit, Martin tells the audience that it's time for his famous nose-on-the-microphone routine. He then leans in and puts his nose on the microphone for several seconds, steps back, takes a long bow, and with gravitas thanks the crowd. "The laugh came not then," he explains, "but only after they realized I had already moved on to the next bit."

It took Martin, by his own estimation, ten years for his new act to cohere, but when it did, he became a monster success. It's clear in his telling that there was no real shortcut to his eventual fame. "[Eventually] you are so experienced [that] there's a confidence that comes out," Martin explained. "I think it's something the audience smells."

Be so good they can't ignore you. When I first heard this advice, I was watching the Martin interview online. It was the winter of 2008 and I was approaching my final year as a graduate student. At the time, I had recently started a blog called Study Hacks, which was inspired by the pair of student-advice guides I had published, and focused mainly on tips for undergraduates. Soon after hearing Martin's axiom, however, I dashed off a blog post that introduced his idea to my readers.[5] "Sure, it's scary," I concluded. "But, even more, I find it liberating."

As my graduate student career had been winding down, I had become obsessed with my research strategy—an obsession that was manifested in the chronic working and reworking of the description of my work on my website. This was a frustrating process: I felt like I was stretching to convince the world that my work was interesting, yet no one cared. Martin's axiom gave me a reprieve from this self-promotion. "Stop focusing on these little details," it told me. "Focus instead on becoming better." Inspired, I turned my attention from my website to a habit that continues to this day: I track the hours spent each month dedicated to thinking hard about research problems (in the month in which I first wrote this chapter, for example, I dedicated forty-two hours to these core tasks).

This hour-tracking strategy helped turn my attention back above all else to the quality of what I produce. At the same time, however, it also felt incremental, as if I hadn't yet grasped the full implications of Martin's radical idea. When I later launched my quest to uncover how people end up loving their work, it didn't take long for me to return to Martin's advice. Intuitively I grasped that it played an important role in constructing a remarkable career. This is what led me to Jordan Tice: If I really wanted to understand this axiom, I figured, I needed to understand the people who live their lives by it.

Listening to Tice talk about his routine, I was struck by his Martin-esque focus on what he produces. As you'll recall, he's happy to spend hours every day, week after week, in a barely furnished monastic room, exhausting himself in pursuit of a new flat-picking technique, all because he thinks it will add something important to the tune he's writing. This dedication to output, I realized, also explains his painful modesty. To Jordan, arrogance doesn't make sense. "Here's what I respect: creating something meaningful and then presenting it to the world," he explained.

Inspired by meeting Jordan, I got in touch with Mark Casstevens to gain a cynical veteran's perspective on the performer's mindset. Mark is a studio musician from Nashville who has certainly earned his stripes: He's played on ninety-nine number one hit singles on the *Billboard* charts. When I told Mark about Jordan, he agreed that an obsessive focus on the quality of what you produce is the rule in professional music. "It trumps your appearance, your equipment, your personality, and your connections," he explained. "Studio musicians have this adage: 'The tape doesn't lie.' Immediately after the recording comes the playback; your ability has no hiding place."

I liked that phrase—*the tape doesn't lie*—as it sums up nicely what motivates performers such as Jordan, Mark, and Steve Martin. If you're not focusing on becoming so good they can't ignore you, you're going to be left behind. This clarity was refreshing.

To simplify things going forward, I'll call this output-centric approach to work **the craftsman mindset**. My goal in Rule #2 is to convince you of an idea that became clearer to me the more time I spent studying performers such as Tice: Irrespective of what type of work you do, the craftsman mindset is *crucial* for building a career you love. Before we get ahead of ourselves, however, I want to take a moment to contrast this mindset with the way most of us are used to thinking about our livelihood.

The Passion Mindset

"[People] thrive by focusing on the question of who they really are—and connecting that to work that they truly love."[6] Po Bronson wrote this in a 2002 manifesto published in *Fast Company*. This should sound familiar, as it's exactly the type of advice you would give if you subscribed to the passion hypothesis, which I debunked in Rule #1. With this in mind, let's call the approach to work endorsed by Bronson **the passion mindset**. Whereas the craftsman mindset focuses on *what you can offer the world,* the passion mindset focuses instead on *what the world can offer you.* This mindset is how most people approach their working lives.

There are two reasons why I dislike the passion mindset (that is, two reasons beyond the fact that, as I argued in Rule #1, it's based on a false premise). First, when you focus only on what your work offers *you,* it makes you hyperaware of what you *don't* like about it, leading to chronic unhappiness. This is especially true for entry-level positions, which, by definition, are not going to be filled with challenging projects and autonomy—these come later. When you enter the working world with the passion mindset, the annoying tasks you're assigned or the frustrations of corporate bureaucracy can become too much to handle.

Second, and more serious, the deep questions driving the passion mindset—"Who am I?" and "What do I truly love?"—are essentially impossible to confirm. "Is this who I really am?" and "Do I love this?" rarely reduce to clear yes-or-no responses. In other words, the passion mindset is almost guaranteed to keep you perpetually unhappy and confused, which probably explains why Bronson admits, not long into his career-seeker epic *What Should I Do With My Life?* that "the one feeling everyone in this book has experienced is of missing out on life."[7]

Adopting the Craftsman Mindset

To summarize, I've presented two different ways people think about their working life. The first is *the craftsman mindset,* which focuses on what you can offer the world. The second is *the passion mindset,* which instead focuses on what the world can offer you. The craftsman · mindset offers clarity, while the passion mindset offers a swamp of ambiguous and unanswerable questions. As I concluded after meeting Jordan Tice, there's something liberating about the craftsman mindset: It asks you to leave behind self-centered concerns about whether your job is "just right," and instead put your head down and plug away at getting really damn good. No one owes you a great career, it argues; you need to earn it—and the process won't be easy.

With this in mind, it's only natural to envy the clarity of performers like Jordan Tice. But here's the core argument of Rule #2: You shouldn't just envy the craftsman mindset, you should *emulate* it. In other words, I am suggesting that you put aside the question of whether your job is your true passion, and instead turn your focus toward becoming so good they can't ignore you. That is, regardless of what you do for a living, approach your work like a true performer.

This shift in mindset proved an exciting development in my own quest. But as I discovered, it comes more easily for some than for others. When I began exploring the craftsman mindset on my blog, some of my readers became uneasy. I noticed them starting to home in on a common counterargument, which I should address before we continue. Here's how one reader put it:

> *Tice is willing to grind out long hours with little recognition, but that's because it's in service to something he's obviously passionate about and has been for a long time. He's found that one job that's right for him.*

I've heard this reaction enough times to give it a name: "the argument from pre-existing passion." At its core is the idea that the craftsman mindset is only viable for those who already feel passionate about their work, and therefore it cannot be presented as an alternative to the passion mindset.

I don't buy it.

First, let's dispense with the notion that performers like Jordan Tice or Steve Martin are perfectly secure in their knowledge that they've found their true calling. If you spend any time with professional entertainers, especially those who are just starting out, one of the first things you notice is their insecurity concerning their livelihood. Jordan had a name for the worries about what his friends are doing with their lives and whether his accomplishments compare favorably: "the cloud of external distractions."

Fighting this cloud is an ongoing battle. Along these lines, Steve Martin was so unsure during his decade-long dedication to improving his routine that he regularly suffered crippling anxiety attacks. The source of these performers' craftsman mindset is not some unquestionable inner passion, but instead something more pragmatic: It's what works in the entertainment business. As Mark Casstevens put it, "the tape doesn't lie": If you're a guitar player or a comedian, what you produce is basically all that matters. If you spend too much time focusing on whether or not you've found your true calling, the question will be rendered moot when you find yourself out of work.

Second, and more fundamental, I don't really care why performers adopt the craftsman mindset. As I mentioned earlier, their world is idiosyncratic, and most of what makes them tick doesn't generalize. The reason I focused on Jordan's story is that I wanted you to see what the craftsman mindset looked like in action. In other words, forget *why* Jordan adopted this mindset and notice instead *how* he deploys it. In the next chapter, I will argue that **regardless of how you feel about your job right now, adopting the craftsman mindset will be the foundation on which you'll build a compelling career**. This is why I reject the "argument from pre-existing passion," because it gets things backward. In reality, as I'll demonstrate, you adopt the craftsman mindset first and *then* the passion follows.

Chapter Five

The Power of Career Capital

*In which I justify the importance of the craftsman
mindset by arguing that the traits that make a great job
great are rare and valuable, and therefore, if you want
a great job, you need to build up rare and valuable
skills—which I call **career capital**—to offer in return.*

The Economics of Great Jobs

In the last chapter I offered a bold proposition: If you
want to love what you do, abandon the *passion mindset*
("what can the world offer me?") and instead adopt the
craftsman mindset ("what can I offer the world?").

My argument for this strategy starts with a simple
question: What makes a great job great? In exploring this
question, it helps to get specific. In Rule #1, I provided
several examples of people who had great jobs and love
(or loved) what they do—so we can draw from there.
Among others, I introduced Apple founder Steve Jobs,
radio host Ira Glass, and master surfboard shaper Al
Merrick. Using this trio as our running example, I can
now ask what it is specifically about these three careers

that makes them so compelling? Here are the answers that I came up with:

TRAITS THAT DEFINE GREAT WORK

- **Creativity**: Ira Glass, for example, is pushing the boundaries of radio, and winning armfuls of awards in the process.
- **Impact**: From the Apple II to the iPhone, Steve Jobs has changed the way we live our lives in the digital age.
- **Control**: No one tells Al Merrick when to wake up or what to wear. He's not expected in an office from nine to five. Instead, his Channel Island Surfboards factory is located a block from the Santa Barbara beach, where Merrick still regularly spends time surfing. (Jake Burton Carpenter, founder of Burton Snowboards, for example, recalls how negotiations for the merger between the two companies happened while he and Merrick waited for waves in a surf lineup.)

This list isn't comprehensive, but if consider your own dream-job fantasies, you'll likely notice some combination of these traits. We can now advance to the question that really matters: How do you get these traits in your own working life? One of the first things I noticed when I began to study this question is that these factors are *rare*. Most jobs don't offer their employees great creativity, impact, or control over what they do and how they do it. If you're a recent college graduate in an entry-level job, for example, you're much more likely to hear "go change the water cooler" than you are "go change the world."

By definition, we also know that these traits are *valuable*—as they're the key to making a job great. But now we're moving into well-trod territory. Basic economic theory tells us that if you want something that's both rare and valuable, you need something rare and valuable to offer in return—this is Supply and Demand 101. It follows that if you want a great job, you need something of great value to offer in return. If this is true, of course, we should see it in the stories of our trio of examples—and we do. Now that we know what to look for, this transactional interpretation of compelling careers becomes suddenly apparent.

Consider Steve Jobs. When Jobs walked into Paul Terrell's Byte Shop he was holding something that was literally rare and valuable: the circuit board for the Apple I, one of the more advanced personal computers in the fledgling market at the time. The money from selling a hundred units of that original design gave Jobs more control in his career, but in classic economic terms, to get even more valuable traits in his working life, he needed to increase the value of what he had to offer. It's at this point that Jobs's ascent begins to accelerate. He takes on $250,000 in funding from Mark Markkula and works with Steve Wozniak to produce a new computer design that is unambiguously too good to be ignored. There were other engineers in the Bay Area's Homebrew Computer Club culture who could match Jobs's and Wozniak's technical skill, but Jobs had the insight to take on investment and to focus this technical energy toward producing a complete product. The result was the Apple II, a machine that leaped ahead of the competition: It had color graphics; the monitor and keyboard were integrated inside the case; the architecture was open, allowing rapid expansion of memory and peripherals (such as the floppy disk, which the Apple II was the first to introduce into mainstream use). This was the product that put the company on the map and that pushed Jobs from a small-time entrepreneur into the head of a visionary company. He produced something of great value and in return his career got an injection of creativity, impact, and control.

The radio host Ira Glass was given the opportunity to create his genre-defining radio show *This American Life* only after he had proven himself as one of public radio's best editors and hosts. Glass started as an intern and then moved on to become a tape cutter for *All Things Considered*. There are many young people who start down the same path as Glass: landing an internship at a local NPR station and then moving up to a low-level production position. But Glass began to break away from the pack when he turned his focus on making his skills more rare and more valuable. The crispness of his segment editing eventually gained him the opportunity to host a few of his own segments on air. And even though Glass has a voice that mocks everything sacred about what a radio personality should sound like, he began to win awards for his segments. It's possible that a latent natural talent for editing may be playing a role here, but recall from Rule #1 that Glass emphasizes the importance of the hard work required to develop skill. "All of us who do creative work...you get into this thing, and there's like a 'gap.' What you're making isn't so good, okay?... It's trying to be good but...it's just not that great," he explained in an interview about his career.[1] "The key thing is to force yourself through the work, force the skills to come; that's the hardest phase," he elaborated in his *Roadtrip Nation* session. In other words, this is not the story of a prodigy who walked into a radio station after college and walked out with a show. The more you read about Glass, the more you encounter a young man who was driven to develop his skills until they were too valuable to be ignored.

This strategy worked. After the success of his short segments for *All Things Considered*, Glass was tapped to cohost a string of different local shows produced out of Chicago's WBEZ station, further increasing the value of his skills. In 1995, when the station manager at WBEZ decided to put together a free-form show with any eye toward national syndication—a show called *This American Life*—Glass was at the top of his list. His career today is rich with creativity, impact, and control, but when you read his story, the economic undertones are unmistakable. Glass exchanged a collection of hard-won, rare, and valuable skills for his fantastic job.

With Al Merrick, not surprisingly, we get the same style of story. The rare and valuable skill that launched Merrick's career as a professional surfboard shaper is crystal clear: His boards won competitions. What's important to note is that this was not always the case. Merrick picked up the trade of fiberglass shaping from his years spent as a boatbuilder, and he knew about surfing from his own on-again, off-again relationship with the sport, but it took an abundance of hard work to get his board-crafting skills to the place where they were valuable. "[Starting out,] a lot of time you're afraid that you're going to be a failure, that this guy you're making a board for is a world champion and his boards [won't be] working right," he recalled in his *Roadtrip Nation* session. "It just makes me work harder and try harder to accomplish what I'm trying to accomplish with a surfboard." Having an office a block from the beach, with the freedom to take off to surf on a moment's notice, sounds great, but it's not the type of job that is just being handed out. To get it, Merrick realized he needed a rare and valuable skill to offer in exchange. Once he had surf pros like Kelly Slater riding his boards—and winning— he became free to dictate the terms of his working life.

Here, then, are the main strands of my argument:

THE CAREER CAPITAL THEORY OF GREAT WORK

- The traits that define great work are rare and valuable.
- Supply and demand says that if you want these traits you need rare and valuable skills to offer in return. Think of these rare and valuable skills you can offer as your **career capital.**
- The craftsman mindset, with its relentless focus on becoming "so good they can't ignore you," is a strategy well suited for acquiring career capital. This is why it trumps the passion mindset if your goal is to create work you love.

Jobs, Glass, and Merrick all adopted the craftsman mindset. (Some even use these exact words in describing themselves. "I was a craftsman," said Merrick, in an interview on his early days as a board shaper.[2]) Career capital theory tells us that this is no coincidence. The traits that define great work require that you have something rare and valuable to offer in return—skills I call career capital. The craftsman mindset, with its relentless focus on what you produce, is *exactly* the mindset you would adopt if your goal was to acquire as much career capital as possible. Ultimately, this is why I promote the craftsman mindset over the passion mindset. This is not some philosophical debate on the existence of passion or the value of hard work—I'm being intensely pragmatic: You need to get good in order to get good things in your working life, and the craftsman mindset is focused on achieving exactly this goal.

But there is, I must admit, a darker corollary to this argument. The passion mindset is not just ineffective for creating work you love; in many cases it can actively work against this goal, sometimes with devastating consequences.

From Courage to Food Stamps

A pair of articles, published within two days of each other in the *New York Times* in the summer of 2009, emphasize the contrast between the passion mindset and the craftsman mindset. The first article concerned Lisa Feuer.[3] At the age of thirty-eight, Feuer quit her career in advertising and marketing. Chafing under the constraints of corporate life, she started to question whether this was her calling. "I'd watched my husband go into business for himself, and I felt like I could do it, too," she said. So she decided to give entrepreneurship a try.

As reported by the *Times*, Feuer enrolled in a two-hundred-hour yoga instruction course, tapping a home equity loan to pay the $4,000 tuition. Certification in hand, she started Karma Kids Yoga, a yoga practice focused on young children and pregnant women. "I love what I do," she told the reporter when justifying the difficulties of starting a freelance business.

The passion mindset supports Feuer's decision. To those enthralled by the myth of a true calling, there's nothing more heroic than trading comfort for passion. Consider, for example, the author Pamela Slim, a believer in the passion mindset who wrote the popular book *Escape from Cubicle Nation*.[4] Slim describes on her website the following sample dialogue, which she claims she has often:

> **Me:** So are you ready to move forward with your plan?
> **Them:** I know what I have to do, but I don't know if I can do it! Who am I to pretend to be a successful (artist) (coach) (consultant) (masseuse)? What if everyone looks at my website and laughs hysterically that I would even consider selling my services? Why would anyone ever want to connect with me?
> **Me:** Time for a little work on your backbone.[5]

Motivated by these encounters, Slim launched a phone-seminar product called *Rebuild Your Backbone*. Its goal is to convince more people to be like Lisa Feuer by finding the courage to follow their dreams. The course description says Slim will answer questions like "Why do we get stuck living other people's models of success?" and "How do we get the courage to do big things in the world?" It costs forty-seven dollars.

Rebuild Your Backbone is an example of the *courage culture*, a growing community of authors and online commentators pushing the following idea: The biggest obstacle between you and work you love is a lack of *courage*—the courage required to step away from "other people's definition of success" and to follow your dream. It's an idea that makes perfect sense when presented against the backdrop of the passion mindset: If there's some perfect job waiting for us out there, every day we're not following this passion is a wasted day. When viewed from this perspective, Feuer's move appears courageous and long overdue; she could be a guest lecturer in Pamela Slim's teleseminar. But this idea crumbles when viewed from the perspective of career capital theory—a perspective that makes Karma Kids Yoga suddenly seem like a poor gamble.

The downside of the passion mindset is that it strips away merit. For passion proponents like Slim, launching a freelance career that gives you control, creativity, and impact is easy—it's just the act of getting started that trips us up. Career capital theory disagrees. It tells us that great work doesn't just require great courage, but also skills of great (and real) value. When Feuer left her advertising career to start a yoga studio, not only did she discard the career capital acquired over many years in the marketing industry, but she transitioned into an unrelated field where she had almost no capital. Given yoga's popularity, a one-month training program places Feuer pretty near the bottom of the skill hierarchy of yoga practitioners, making her a long way from being so good she can't be ignored. According to career capital theory, she therefore has very little leverage in her yoga-working life. It's unlikely, therefore, that things will go well for Feuer—which, unfortunately, is exactly what ended up happening.

As the recession hit in 2008, Feuer's business struggled. One of the gyms where she taught closed. Then two classes she offered at a local public high school were dropped, and with the tightening economy, demands for private lessons diminished. In 2009, when she was profiled for the *Times*, she was on track to make only $15,000 for the year. Toward the conclusion of the profile, Feuer sends the reporter a text message: "I'm at the food stamp office now, waiting." It's signed: "Sent from my iPhone."

Two days after Lisa Feuer's profile was published, the *Times* introduced its readers to another marketing executive, Joe Duffy.[6] Like Feuer, Duffy worked in advertising and eventually began to chafe at the constraints of corporate life. "I was tired of the agency business," he recalls. "I [wanted] to simplify my life and focus on the creative side again." Given that Duffy's original training was as an artist—he had entered the advertising industry as a technical illustrator only after he had a hard time making a living with his paintings—supporters of the passion mindset might encourage someone in Duffy's situation to leave advertising behind and return to his passion for the creative arts.

Duffy, it turns out, is from the craftsman school of thought. Instead of fleeing the constraints of his current job, he began acquiring the career capital he'd need to buy himself out of them. His specialty became international logos and brand icons. As his ability grew, so did his options. Eventually, he was hired away by the Minneapolis-based Fallon McElligott agency, which allowed him to run his own subsidiary within the larger organization, calling it Duffy Designs. In other words, his capital had bought him more autonomy.

After twenty years at Fallon McElligott, working on logos for major companies such as Sony and Coca-Cola, Duffy once again invested his capital to gain more autonomy, this time by starting his own fifteen-person shop: Duffy & Partners. This entrepreneurial move contrasts sharply with Feuer's. Duffy started his own company with enough career capital to immediately thrive—he was one of the world's best logo men and had a waiting list of clients. Feuer started her company with only two hundred hours of training and an abundance of courage.

It's fair to guess that by the time Duffy recently retired, he loved what he did. His work gave him heaps of control and respect and, depending on your view of the importance of advertising, also had a great impact on the world. To me, however, the most vivid contrast to Feuer's story was Duffy's purchase of Duffy Trails, a hundred-acre retreat on the banks of Wisconsin's Totagatic River. Duffy is an avid cross-country skier, and the five miles of wooded trails, skiable from November through March, made the retreat irresistible. As reported by the *New York Times,* the property can comfortably house at least twenty guests, spread over three different residential outbuildings, but on the hottest summer nights, it's the screened gazebo by the retreat's sixteen-acre, bass-stocked lake that attracts the most visitors.

Duffy purchased this property at the age of forty-five: in other words, not long after the age at which Feuer left advertising to pursue her yoga business. It's this parallel that gives this pair of stories their Frostian undertones. "Two roads diverged in a yellow wood," and one traveler chose the path to mastery while the other was called toward passion's glow. The former ended up celebrated in the industry, in control of his own livelihood, and weekending with his family in a forested retreat. The latter ended up on food stamps.

This comparison is not necessarily fair. We don't know that Feuer could have replicated Duffy's success if she had stayed in marketing and advertising and had focused her restless energy on becoming excellent. But as a metaphor, the story works nicely. The image of

Feuer, waiting in line for food stamps, while Duffy, at a similar age, returns from a successful overseas trip to spend a relaxing weekend skiing at Duffy Trails, is striking. It captures well both the risk and the illogic of starting from scratch as contrasted with the leverage gained by instead acquiring more career capital. Both Feuer and Duffy had the same issues with their work; these issues emerged at around the same time; and they both had the same desire to love what they do. But they had two different approaches to tackling these issues. In the end, it was Duffy's commitment to craftsmanship that was the obvious winner.

When Craftsmanship Fails

Not long before I started writing this chapter, I received an e-mail from John, a recent college graduate and long-time reader of my blog. He was concerned about his new job as a tax consultant. Though he found the work to be "sometimes interesting," the hours were long and the tasks were fiercely prescribed, making it difficult to stand out. "Aside from not liking the lifestyle," John complained, "I'm concerned that my work doesn't serve a larger purpose, and, in fact, that it actively hurts the most vulnerable."

This chapter has argued in favor of the craftsman mindset and against its passion-centric alternative. Part of what makes the craftsman mindset thrilling is its agnosticism toward the type of work you do. The traits that define great work are bought with career capital, the theory argues; they don't come from matching your work to your innate passion. Because of this, you don't have to sweat whether you've found your calling—most any work can become the foundation for a compelling career. John had heard this argument and wrote me because he was having a hard time applying it to his life as a tax consultant. He didn't like his work and he wanted to know if, like a good craftsman, he should just suck it up and continue to focus on getting good. This is an important question, and here's what I told John:

"It sounds like you should leave your job." On reflection, it became clear to me that certain jobs are better suited for applying career capital theory than others. To aid John, I ended up devising a list of three traits that disqualify a job as providing a good foundation for building work you love:

THREE DISQUALIFIERS FOR APPLYING THE CRAFTSMAN MINDSET

1. The job presents few opportunities to distinguish yourself by developing relevant skills that are rare and valuable.
2. The job focuses on something you think is useless or perhaps even actively bad for the world.
3. The job forces you to work with people you really dislike.[7]

A job with any combination of these disqualifying traits can thwart your attempts to build and invest career capital. If it satisfies the first trait, skill growth isn't possible. If it satisfies the second two traits, then even though you *could* build up reserves of career capital, you'll have a hard time sticking around long enough to accomplish this goal. John's job satisfied the first two traits, so he needed to leave.

To give another example: As a computer scientist at MIT, which I was while writing this book, I got quite a few e-mails from Wall Street headhunters. They were hiring for jobs that provide plenty of room to develop skills and they're not afraid to compensate you well for your time. "There is a small handful of firms on Wall Street that pay better than everyone else, about three or four of them," said one headhunter who wrote me recently. "This company is one of them." (I was later told by friends that the starting salary for these firms was in the two to three hundred thousand dollar range.) But to me, these firms satisfy the second condition listed above. This realization allowed me to confidently delete these offers as they arrived.

The big-picture point worth noting here, however, is that these disqualifying traits still have nothing to do with whether a job is the right fit for some innate passion. They remain much more general. Working right, therefore, still trumps finding the right work.

Now that I've made my pitch for the craftsman mindset, and moderated it with the exceptions listed above, it's time to see it in action.

Chapter Six

The Career Capitalists

In which I demonstrate the power of career capital in action with two profiles of people who leveraged the craftsman mindset to construct careers they love.

Two Career Capitalists

Alex Berger is thirty-one: He's a successful television writer and he loves his work. Mike Jackson is twenty-nine: He's a cleantech venture capitalist and he also loves his work. This chapter is dedicated to telling their stories, as they both highlight the somewhat messy reality of using the craftsman mindset to generate fantastic livelihoods. Alex and Mike both focused on getting good—not finding their passion—and then used the career capital this generated to acquire the traits that made their careers compelling.

The Closed-Off World of Television Kabillionaires

Let's assume for the moment that you want to be hired as a television writer on a network series. Your first step is to get past someone like Jamie.

Jamie, who is in his late twenties, was recently involved in the writer-staffing process for a network show. He agreed to provide me a glimpse into his world so long as I kept him and his show anonymous. Here's what I learned: TV writing is not an easy gig to land. According to Jamie, the process unfolds as follows. First, the producers put out a call to talent agencies to send over sample scripts from their writers. For his particular show, Jamie received around a hundred packages, each containing a sample script, which Jamie read, reviewed, and graded. Only around the best twenty or so from this pile will be passed on to the producers for additional consideration. Keep in mind that the producers have already hired their favored veteran writers, so there are precious few spots left to be filled from this open call.

To provide a sense of the competitiveness of this process, Jamie sent me a copy of his script evaluations. Out of the hundred or so writers who submitted scripts, all but fourteen sent a script that had already been produced and aired on television. Of the fourteen who had not yet broken into the industry, the highest score any received from Jamie was a 6.5 out of 10. Most of this group, however, fared much worse. "It was flat, without any interesting storytelling, engaging act-outs, or smart dialogue," he wrote about one such script (score: 4 out of 10). "I only read about a quarter of this script but it's clearly pretty subpar," he said about another.

In other words, getting on the inside in the world of

television writing is daunting. But at the same time, I can understand why so many thousands aspire to this goal: It's a fantastic job. For one thing, there's the money. As a new writer, your salary starts modest. The Writer's Guild of America guarantees that you make at least $2,500 a week, which, given a standard twenty-six week season, is decent for half a year of work. Depending on the success of the series, you'll then progress after a year or two to become a story editor, where, as a longtime TV writer explained in a Salon.com article on the topic, "you're still making shit" (though, as another writer admitted, "shit" at this point qualifies as over $10,000 an episode).[1] Things start to get interesting when you make it to the next level: producer. Once there, "you're in the money." Top writers can pull in seven-figure paychecks. In the Salon.com article referenced above, the term "kabillionaire" was used by multiple people to describe the salaries of producers on long-running shows.

Of course, you can also make lots of money in other jobs. A fast riser at Goldman Sachs can hit the seven-figure mark (including bonuses) by his or her midthirties, and a partner at a prestigious law firm can get somewhere similar a few years later. But the difference between Wall Street and Hollywood in the style of work is staggering. Imagine: no e-mail, no late-night contract negotiations, no need to master intricate bond markets or legal precedents. As a writer your whole focus is on one thing: telling good stories. The work can be intense, as you're often under deadline to deliver the next script, but it only lasts half a year, and it's immensely creative, and you can wear shorts, and the catered food, as was emphasized to me several times, is fantastic. ("Writers are crazy about their food," one source explained.) To recast the job in the terms I introduced in the last chapter, television writing is attractive because it has the three traits that make people love their work: impact, creativity, and control.

By the time I met him, Alex Berger had managed to break into this elite world. He had recently sold a pilot to USA Network. To sell a pilot is to sell an idea: You sit down in a room with three or four executives from the network and spend five minutes pitching your vision. At a cable network like USA, these executives will hear around fifteen to twenty such pitches a week. They then retreat to a staff meeting and choose three or four to actually buy. Alex's idea was one of the four they bought that week.

Alex has a few more hurdles to leap before his show makes it on the air at USA, but selling a pilot, by itself, is seen as impressive in the industry—a mark that you know what you're doing. As if to emphasize this impressiveness, one of the executives at USA, who liked Alex's work, helped staff him on an already running show, the hit spy drama *Covert Affairs*, so that he'd have something to do while waiting for the pilot decisions to be made. Not that Alex needed the boost to his reputation:

He had already written and aired episodes for three different shows leading up to this point. His latest gig was on the stop-motion comedy *Glenn Martin, DDS*, which he had cocreated with Michael Eisner and had run for two seasons. In other words, there's no doubt that Alex is an established writer in an industry that allows few through its gates.

The question is, how did he do it?

How Alex Berger Broke into Hollywood

What makes television a hard industry to crack is the fact that it's a winner-take-all market. There's only one type of career capital here, the quality of your writing, and there are thousands of hopefuls trying to gain enough of this capital to impress a very small group of buyers.

In this respect, however, Alex had an advantage. At Dartmouth College he had been a debater, and a damn good one at that: In 2002 his two-man team arrived at the National Debate Tournament with the country's highest rank; Alex then went on to win the Best Speaker prize at the tournament. In debate, as in television writing, there's no mystery about what separates good from bad: The scoring system is specific and known. To become the country's best debater, therefore, Alex had to master the art of continual improvement. Hearing the story of how he then went on to succeed in Hollywood convinced me that it was exactly this skill that fueled his fast rise.

When Alex made the decision to move to Hollywood, his logic, in typical debater fashion, was airtight: "I figured I could always apply to law school," he recalled thinking, "but realistically this would be my only chance to try out writing." Alex admits that when he first moved west he wasn't even sure what his goals were: "I had a number of things I wanted to do, but didn't know what they meant. I thought I wanted to be a network executive, for example, but had no idea what that involved. I thought I might be a TV writer, but didn't know what that meant either." This was not a classic case of the young man building the courage to follow his unmistakable passion.

When Alex first arrived in LA, he took a job as website editor for the *National Lampoon*. Once there, he discovered that the *Lampoon* was also interested in television production. Drawing from the adage "write what you know," Alex pitched them *Master Debaters*, a show that required comedians to debate humorous topics in front of a panel of judges. He was given a modest amount of money to film a pilot, which he did, in a Border's bookstore in Westwood. But making television shows is a tough game, and the *National Lampoon*'s tentative effort didn't go anywhere.

What I like about Alex's story is what he does next: He quit his job at the *National Lampoon* and took a position as an assistant to a development executive at NBC. It's here that I see Alex's debater instincts stir back to life. The *National Lampoon* was too far to the periphery of the industry to teach him what it takes to succeed. By accepting an assistant position he threw himself into the center of the action, where he could find out how things *actually* work.

It didn't take long for Alex to discover what allows some writers to succeed in catching the attention of a network while so many others fail: *They write good scripts*—a task that's more difficult than many imagine. Spurred by this insight, Alex turned his attention to writing. *Lots of writing.* During the eight months he spent as an assistant he dedicated his nights to working on a trio of different writing projects. First, before Alex left the *National Lampoon*, they had optioned his *Master Debaters* idea to VH1—while an assistant Alex was still polishing the script for the VH1 version of the pilot. (In the end, like most pilots, nothing ever came of the VH1 option.) At the same time, he was working on a pilot for an unrelated show along with a producer he had met at the *Lampoon*. And on his own, he was writing a screenplay about his life growing up in Washington, D.C. "I might finish writing at two or three A.M., then have to leave at eight the next morning to get back to my job at NBC on time," Alex recalls. It was a busy period.

After eight months as an assistant, Alex heard about a job opening for a script assistant on *Commander in Chief*, a *West Wing* copycat helmed by Geena Davis. He jumped at the chance to observe professional TV writ-

ers up close, even though it was still a low-level position. On the side, he also added to his portfolio a spec
script-in-progress for the HBO series *Curb Your Enthusiasm*, aggressively seeking feedback on his early drafts. "I
thought I needed more samples to get work," he recalls.

While working as a script assistant for *Commander
in Chief*, Alex started to pitch episode ideas to the room:
One of the privileges of being a script assistant is that
you can always get a (quick) consideration of your pitch.
Not long before the show was canceled, he finally caught
the attention of the room with an episode idea about lost
missiles from a plane crash in Pakistan and the politi-
cal fallout of a gay commitment ceremony. Working with
Cynthia Cohen, one of the staff writers on the show, he
produced a draft of the episode.

"For those with free TiVo space, I recommend giving
the 'thumbs up' to a groundbreaking episode of *Commander in Chief*, this Thursday at ten," Alex wrote in an
e-mail to friends around this time. "Why groundbreaking, you ask? Because, within the first ten minutes, for
the first time in the history of network television, the
words 'Alex' and 'Berger' will appear—in succession,
mind you—just underneath the words 'written by.'"

With his first produced television script now in
hand, things began to move quickly for Alex. After *Commander in Chief* was canceled, he took another low-level
job, this time working with the producer Jonathan Lisco
in the run-up for his new show, *K-Ville*, a post-Katrina

New Orleans drama being developed for Fox. Given his writing credit, however, and a collection of increasingly polished spec scripts, this job became an informal tryout for Alex: He was given the chance to impress Lisco—which he did. When a spot opened on the writing staff for *K-Ville*, it was given to Alex: his first official position as a staff writer. He went on to write and air two episodes before the show was canceled.

After *K-Ville*, a mutual friend set up a meeting between Alex and Michael Eisner, who, fresh from leaving Disney, was looking to create a television comedy as his first project as an independent producer. Alex got the meeting because he was a former staff writer for a network show, but it was his *Curb Your Enthusiasm* script that convinced Eisner to ask him to write a pilot for his new idea. Eisner liked the pilot draft, and Alex went on to help him cocreate the show, *Glenn Martin, DDS*, which aired for two seasons as a flagship program for Nickelodeon's "Nick at Night" block.

It was as *Glenn Martin* was winding down that Alex sold his pilot to USA and was staffed on one of their hit shows, *Covert Affairs*—the setting where I first introduced him to you.

Alex's Capital

To understand Alex Berger's various breaks, you need to understand the career capital that enabled them. For example, it was certainly a big deal for Michael Eisner to ask Alex to help him create a show, but think about what this break required: At the time, Alex had been a staff writer for a network show and had a quality-comedy spec script—polished over many rounds of aggressive feedback—in his portfolio. That's an important collection of capital.

If you rewind the clock more and ask how Alex got a staff spot on *K-Ville*, you once again discover a capital transaction: He had already written and aired an episode of another network drama, *Commander in Chief.* Another important collection of capital.

Rewind the clock further and ask how Alex, as a lowly script assistant, got a script aired on *Commander in Chief,* and you encounter the writing skill he had developed over the previous years spent obsessively honing his craft—a period where he was often working on three or four scripts at a time, always seeking feedback for how he could make them better. The Alex Berger who first arrived in LA, fresh out of college, did not have this writing-skill capital. By the time he was working for *Commander in Chief,* however, he was ready for his first major transaction.

In this telling, the story of Alex's fast rise is not one of passion triumphing over setbacks: It's much less dramatic. Alex, the former debate champion, coolly assessed what career capital was valuable in this market. He then set out with the intensity once reserved for debate prep to acquire this capital as fast as possible. What this story lacks in pizazz, it makes up in repeatability: There's nothing mysterious about how Alex Berger broke into Hollywood—he simply understood the value, and difficulty, of becoming good.

The Most Desirable Job in Silicon Valley

Mike Jackson is a director at the Westly Group, a cleantech venture capital firm on Silicon Valley's famous Sand Hill Road. To say that Mike has a desirable job is an understatement. "I have a friend who recently had dinner with the dean in charge of a top-tier business school," he told me. "And at this dinner, the dean said that everyone in their graduating class right now wants to be a cleantech VC." Mike has experienced this firsthand: He receives dozens of e-mails from business school students asking him about his path. He used to try to answer them, but now, due to time constraints, he mostly ignores them. "Everyone wants my job," he explained.

The fact that people covet his position isn't surprising. Clean energy is hot. It's a way to help the world while at the same time, as Mike admitted, "you make a lot of money." In his position, Mike has traveled the world, met senators, and spent time with the mayors of both Sacramento and Los Angeles. During one of our conversations, he mentioned that David Plouffe, Barack

Obama's campaign manager, had been "hanging around the office."

What interests me about Mike is that, like Alex Berger, he didn't arrive at his outstanding job by following a clear passion. Instead he carefully and persistently gathered career capital, confident that valuable skills would translate into valuable opportunities. Unlike Alex, however, Mike started gathering capital *before* he knew what he wanted to do with it. In fact, he had never given a moment's thought to cleantech venture capital until a couple weeks before his first interview.

How Mike Jackson Became a Venture Capitalist

Mike majored in biology and earth systems at Stanford. After earning his bachelor's degree, Mike elected to stay for a fifth year to earn a master's. The professor who supervised his master's was trying to decide whether or not to launch a major research project studying the natural-gas sector in India, so he arranged Mike's thesis to act as an exploration of the project's viability. In the fall of 2005, after Mike finished his graduate degree, his supervisor decided he liked what he saw and launched the major research project. Not surprisingly, he asked Mike to help him lead it—at this point, Mike had just spent a year getting up to speed on its details.

Mike, who is competitive by nature, tackled the

project with intensity, driven by the belief that the better he did now, the better his options would be later. "During this time, I traveled to India ten times and to China four to five times, in addition to quite a bit of travel in Europe," he recalls. "I met with the heads of major utilities, and I learned how the global energy market *really* works." When the project concluded in the fall of 2007, Mike and his professor held a major international conference to release and discuss the results. Academics and government officials from around the world attended.

With the project complete, Mike had to decide what to do next. Of the many valuable skills he picked up from the project, one in particular was a "deep understanding" of how the international carbon market works. As part of this expertise, he learned that the United States had an obscure exchange, known as the renewable energy credits market. "Almost no one understood these things; it was a really fractured market with huge information asymmetry," he recalls. Being one of the few people who actually knew how this market worked, Mike decided to start a business. He called it Village Green. The idea was simple: You give money to Mike, he does complicated transactions that only he and a few other energy regulation wonks really understand, and then he offers you certification that you've purchased enough carbon offsets for your business to be deemed carbon neutral.

Mike ran this business for two years along with a friend from Stanford and a rotating series of other partners. They were headquartered in a rental house not far from where he lived in San Francisco. The company never struggled to pay its expenses, but it also never became a thriving concern. So when the economy went sour in 2009, Mike and his partner decided to shutter it instead of hunkering down and trying to ride out the recession.

"We decided to get real jobs," is how Mike describes what happened next. Here's how the process unfolded: A stand-up comedian friend of Mike's had a girlfriend who was interviewing at a venture capital firm. She decided not to take the job, but recommended that they talk to Mike. "She thought I would be a good fit for venture capital, given my experience with my company," he said. Mike knew that he was not a good match for this technology-focused fund. "I have no idea how to find the next Facebook," he told me, "but I could tell you if a solar energy firm was probably going to make money." He figured, however, that since he had never been through a real job interview before, the experience would provide good practice.

"The interview was pretty low-key, because we both realized early on I wasn't going to get this job, but we hit it off on a personal level" he recalls. At some point in the discussion, the venture capitalist had an idea. "You know, you would be a good match for this cleantech fund that's starting up," he said. "Why don't I introduce you to my friend over there?"

In the summer of 2009, Mike started a trial period as an intern at the Westly Group. In October they gave him a full-time position as an analyst, and soon after, he was promoted to associate. Two years later he became a director. "When people ask me how I got my job," he now jokes, "I tell them to make friends with a comedian."

Mike's Capital

Mike Jackson leveraged the craftsman mindset to do whatever he did really well, thus ensuring that he came away from each experience with as much career capital as possible. He never had elaborate plans for his career. Instead, after each working experience, he would stick his head up to see who was interested in his newly expanded store of capital, and then jump at whatever opportunity seemed most promising.

One could argue that luck also played an important role in Mike's story. He was, for example, lucky to find a personal connection to a venture capitalist and then to hit it off when they met in person. But these types of small breaks are common. What mattered most in Mike's story is that once he stumbled through the door, his career capital went to work getting him a fantastic job offer.

If you spend time around Mike, you quickly realize how serious he is about doing what he does well. It's true that he now loves his work, but he's still quick to turn the conversation back to *how* he approaches it. As you'll learn more about in the next chapter, Mike literally tracks every hour of his day, down to quarter-hour increments, on a spreadsheet. He wants to ensure that his attention is focused on the activities that matter. "It's so easy to just come in and spend your whole day on e-mail," he warned. On the sample spreadsheet he sent me, he allots himself only ninety minutes per day for e-mail. The day before we last spoke he had only spent forty-five. This is a man who is serious about doing what he does really well.

In the end, Mike's focus on capabilities over callings obviously paid off. He has a fantastic job, but it was one that required a fantastic store of career capital to be offered in exchange.

Chapter Seven

Becoming a Craftsman

*In which I introduce **deliberate practice**, the key strategy for acquiring career capital, and show how to integrate it into your own working life.*

Why Is Jordan Tice a Better Guitar Player than Me?

Jordan Tice and I both started playing guitar at the age of twelve. After receiving my first guitar, I formed a band and several months later performed my first "concert"— a reduced-speed interpretation of Nirvana's "All Apologies," played to polite applause at the Tollgate Grammar School sixth-grade talent show. After this I got serious: I took lessons throughout junior high school and high school. I played every day—sometimes rocking blues solos to Hendrix recordings for hours at a time. My band, which had the questionable name of Rocking Chair, played around a dozen shows a year: festivals, parties, competitions—anywhere, really, that people would allow us to set up our equipment. We once played a gig in a graveyard facing a parking lot. Our drummer's mom videotaped it. When she pans the camera from our setup in front of the graves to the lot, you realize that the "crowd" consists of no more than a dozen people on folding chairs. She still finds it funny to play this tape.

By the time I graduated high school I could play from a repertoire of hundreds of songs, ranging from Green Day to Pink Floyd. In other words, I had reached the level of expertise you would expect from someone who had played an instrument seriously for the last six years. But this is what I find fascinating: Compared to Jordan Tice's ability at this same age, I was mediocre.

Jordan picked up guitar at the same point in his life as I did. But by the time *he* graduated high school, he had been touring the mid-Atlantic with a group of professional bluegrass musicians and had signed his first record deal. When I was in high school, the acoustic group Nickel Creek was thought of, admiringly, by my grade's music snobs as Dave Matthews for cool people. When Jordan was in high school, he regularly played gigs with their bass player, Mark Schatz. The question hanging over this comparison is why, even though we had both played seriously for the same amount of time, did I end up an average high school strummer while Jordan became a star?

It didn't take long into my visit with Jordan to understand the answer to this question. The difference in our abilities by the age of eighteen had less to do with the number of hours we practiced—though he probably racked up more total practice hours than I did, we weren't all that far apart—and more to do with what we did with those hours. One of my most vivid memories of Rocking Chair, for example, was my discomfort playing anything I didn't know real well. There's a mental strain that accompanies feeling your way though a tune that's not ingrained in muscle memory, and I hated that feeling. I learned songs reluctantly, then clung to them fiercely once they had become easy for me. I used to get upset when our rhythm guitar player would suggest we try out something new during band practice. He was happy glancing at a chord chart and then jumping in. I wasn't. Even at that young age I realized that my discomfort with mental discomfort was a liability in the performance world.

Compare this to Jordan's earliest experiences with the guitar. His first teacher was a friend from his parents' church. As Jordan remembers, their lessons focused on picking out the leads from Allman Brothers records. "So he would write out the lead and then you would go memorize them?" I asked. "No, we would just figure them out by ear," Jordan replied. To the high school version of myself, the idea of learning complicated lead parts by ear would have been way past my threshold of mental strain and patience. But Jordan came to enjoy this labor. In our interview, a decade beyond his high school years, Jordan at one point grabbed his old Martin and knocked off the solo from "Jessica," which he somehow still remembered. "Great melody," he said.

Not only did Jordan's early practice require him to constantly stretch himself beyond what was comfortable, but it was also accompanied by instant feedback. The teacher was always there, Jordan explained, "to jump in and show me if I junked up a harmony."

Watching Jordan's current practice regime, these traits—strain and feedback—remain central. To get up to speed on the wide picking style he needs for his new tune, he keeps adjusting the speed of his practicing to a point just past where he's comfortable. When he hits a wrong note, he immediately stops and starts over, providing instant feedback for himself. While practicing, the strain on his face and the gasping nature of his breaths can be uncomfortable even to *watch*—I can't imagine what it feels like to actually do. But Jordan is happy to practice like this for hours at a time.

This, then, explains why Jordan left me in the dust. I played. But he practiced. The Nashville studio musician Mark Casstevens seconded this dedication to constantly stretching your abilities. When I talked to him, for example, he was in the process of slowly getting up to speed on a "complicated new tune in B-flat with a great deal of barre chords and nasty counterpoint." Even someone with Casstevens's level of (literally) award-winning experience (the Academy of Country Music recently named him Specialty Instrumentalist of the Year) can't avoid the need to "go out to the woodshed in order to practice."

"I develop muscle memory the hard way, by repetition,"

he said, echoing Jordan's long, skill-stretching practice sessions. "The harder I work, the more relaxed I can play, and the better it sounds."

These observations, of course, are about more than just guitar playing. The central idea of this chapter is that **the difference in strategy that separates average guitar players like me from stars like Tice and Casstevens is not confined to music.** This focus on stretching your ability and receiving immediate feedback provides the core of a more universal principle—one that I increasingly came to believe provides the key to successfully acquiring career capital in almost any field.

How to Become a Grand Master

If you want to understand the science of how people get good at something, chess is an excellent place to start. For one thing, it provides a clear definition of ability: your ranking. Though different chess ranking systems have been proposed with varying popularity, the current standard is the Elo system used by the World Chess Federation. This system gives players a score starting at zero that increases as they get better. Its calculation is complicated, but at a high level of approximation it reflects one's performance at official tournaments. If you do better than expected, it goes up, and if you do worse, it goes down. A solid novice player who plays the occasional weekend competition will have a score in the triple digits. Bobby Fischer peaked at 2785. In 1990, Garry Kasparov became the first player to ever reach 2800. The highest score ever obtained was 2851, also by Kasparov.

The other reason chess proves useful for studying performance is the fact that it's really hard. To beat Garry Kasparov in 1997, for example, IBM's Deep Blue super-computer had to analyze 200 million moves per second, and to play a competitive opening, it drew from a data-base of over 700,000 grand-master games. Given chess's difficulty, we can expect that the strategies required to get good will be more pronounced and therefore easier to identify.

These traits explain why scientists have been study-ing chess players since as early as the 1920s, when a trio of German psychologists set out to determine if grand masters had freakish memories.[1] (Interestingly, it turns out they don't: Though grand masters are fantastically efficient at storing *chess* positions in their minds, their general recall ability is quite average.) One study that proves especially relevant to our interests is more recent. In 2005, a research team led by Neil Charness, a psychol-ogist from Florida State University, published the results of a decades-long investigation of the practice habits of chess players.[2] Throughout the nineties, Charness's team had been placing ads in newspapers and posting fly-ers at chess tournaments, looking for ranked players to participate in their project. They ended up surveying over four hundred players, from around the world, in an effort to understand why some were better than others. Each player was given a form to fill out that requested a detailed history of the player's chess instruction. The respondents were asked, in essence, to re-create a time line of their development as chess players: At what age did they start? What type of training did they receive at each year? How many tournaments did they play? Were they coached? How much? And so on.

Previous studies had shown it takes around ten years, at minimum, to become a grand master. (As the psychologist K. Anders Ericsson likes to point out, even prodigies like Bobby Fisher managed to fit in ten years of playing before they achieved international recognition: He just started this accumulation earlier than most.) This is the "ten-year rule," sometimes called the "10,000-hour rule," which has been bouncing around scientific circles since the 1970s, but was popularized more recently by Malcolm Gladwell's bestselling 2008 book, *Outliers*.[3] Here's how he summarized it:

The 10,000-Hour Rule

The idea that excellence at performing a complex task requires a critical minimum level of practice surfaces again and again in studies of expertise. In fact, researchers have settled on what they believe is the magic number for true expertise: **ten thousand hours** *[emphasis mine].*

In *Outliers*, Gladwell pointed to this rule as evidence that great accomplishment is not about natural talent, but instead about being in the right place at the right time to accumulate such a massive amount of practice. Bill Gates? He happened to attend one of the first high schools in the country to install a computer and allow their students unsupervised access—making him one of the first in his generation to build up thousands of hours of practice on this technology. Mozart? His dad was a fanatic about practicing. By the time Mozart was being toured around Europe as a prodigy, he had squeezed in more than twice the number of practice hours that similarly aged musician contemporaries had acquired.

What interests me about Charness's study, however, is that it moves beyond the 10,000-hour rule by asking not just *how long* people worked, but also *what type* of work they did. In more detail, they studied players who had all spent roughly the same amount of time—around 10,000 hours—playing chess. Some of these players had become grand masters while others remained at an intermediate level. Both groups had practiced the same amount of time, so the difference in their ability must depend on how they used these hours. It was these differences that Charness sought.

In the 1990s, this was a relevant question. There was debate in the chess world at the time surrounding the best strategies for improving. One camp thought *tournament play* was crucial, as it provides practice with tight time limits and working through distractions. The other camp, however, emphasized *serious study*—pouring over books and using teachers to help identify and then eliminate weaknesses. When surveyed, the participants in Charness's study thought tournament play was probably the right answer. The participants, as it turns out, were wrong. Hours spent in serious study of the game was not just the most important factor in predicting chess skill, it *dominated* the other factors. The researchers discovered that the players who became grand masters spent *five times more hours* dedicated to serious study than those who plateaued at an intermediate level. The grand masters, on average, dedicated around 5,000 hours out of their 10,000 to serious study. The intermediate players, by contrast, dedicated only around 1,000 to this activity.

On closer examination, the importance of serious study becomes more obvious. In serious study, Charness concluded, "materials can be deliberately chosen or adapted such that the problems to be solved are at a level that is appropriately challenging." This contrasts with tournament play, where you are likely to draw an opponent who is either demonstrably better or demonstrably worse than yourself: both situations where "skill improvement is likely to be minimized." Furthermore, in serious study, feedback is immediate: be it from looking up the answer to a chess problem in a book or, as is more typically the case for serious players, receiving immediate feedback from an expert coach. The Norwegian chess phenom Magnus Carlsen, for example, paid Garry Kasparov over $700,000 a year to add polish to his otherwise intuitive playing style.

Notice how well chess fits with our earlier discussion of guitar practice. The "serious study" employed by top chess players sounds similar to Jordan Tice's approach to music: They're both focused on difficult activities, carefully chosen to stretch your abilities where they most need stretching and that provide immediate feedback. At the same time, notice how chess-tournament play sounds a lot like my approach to guitar: It's enjoyable and exciting, but it's not necessarily making you better. I spent many hours playing songs I knew, including dozens and dozens of hours spent on stage. Like the intermediate players in the Charness study, I was letting this satisfying work pile up ineffectively while Jordan, during these same ages, was painstakingly squirreling away the serious study that would make him exceptional.

In the early 1990s, Anders Ericsson, a colleague of Neil Charness at Florida State University, coined the term "deliberate practice" to describe this style of serious study, defining it formally as an "activity designed, typically by a teacher, for the sole purpose of effectively improving specific aspects of an individual's performance."[4] As hundreds of follow-up studies have since shown, deliberate practice provides the key to excellence in a diverse array of fields, among which are chess, medicine, auditing, computer programming, bridge, physics, sports, typing, juggling, dance, and music.[5] If you want to understand the source of professional athletes' talent, for example, look to their practice schedules—almost without exception they have been systematically stretching their athletic abilities, with the guidance of expert coaches, since they were children. If you instead turned the tables on Malcolm Gladwell, and asked him about his writing ability, he too would point you toward deliberate practice. In *Outliers* he notes that he spent ten years honing his craft in the *Washington Post* newsroom before he moved to the *New Yorker* and began writing his breakout book, *The Tipping Point.*

"When experts exhibit their superior performance in public their behavior looks so effortless and natural that we are tempted to attribute it to special talents," Ericsson notes. "However, when scientists began measuring the experts' supposedly superior powers...no general superiority was found."[6] In other words, outside a handful of extreme examples—such as the height of professional basketball players and the girth of football linemen—scientists have failed to find much evidence of natural abilities explaining experts' successes. It is a lifetime accumulation of deliberate practice that again and again ends up explaining excellence.

Here's what struck me as important about deliberate practice: It's not obvious. Outside of fields such as chess, music, and professional athletics, which have clear competitive structures and training regimes, few participate in anything that even remotely approximates this style of skill development. As Ericsson explains, "Most individuals who start as active professionals...change their behavior and increase their performance for a limited time until they reach an acceptable level. Beyond this point, however, further improvements appear to be unpredictable and the number of years of work...is a poor predictor of attained performance." Put another way, **if you just show up and work hard, you'll soon hit a performance plateau beyond which you fail to get any better**. This is what happened to me with my guitar playing, to the chess players who stuck to tournament play, and to most knowledge workers who simply put in the hours: We all hit plateaus.

When I first encountered the work of Ericsson and Charness, this insight startled me. It told me that in most types of work—that is, work that doesn't have a clear training philosophy—most people are stuck. This generates an exciting implication. Let's assume you're a knowledge worker, which is a field without a clear training philosophy. If you can figure out how to integrate deliberate practice into your own life, you have the possibility of blowing past your peers in your value, as you'll likely be alone in your dedication to systematically getting better. That is, *deliberate practice might provide the key to quickly becoming so good they can't ignore you.*

To successfully adopt the craftsman mindset, therefore, we have to approach our jobs in the

**same way that Jordan approaches his guitar play-
ing or Garry Kasparov his chess training—with a
dedication to deliberate practice**. How to accomplish
this feat is the goal of the remainder of this chapter. I want
to start, in the next section, by arguing that I'm not the
first to have this insight. When we return to the stories
of Alex Berger and Mike Jackson, we find that deliberate
practice was at the core of their quest for work they love.

Alex Berger Craves Criticism and
Mike Jackson Doesn't Check E-mail

Consider Alex Berger's two-year rise from assistant to
cocreator of a national television series. He told me that
getting your writing to "network quality" can take from
a couple of years at the minimum to as many as twenty-
five. The reason he was on the fast track, he explained,
was his debate-champ-style obsession with improving.
"I have a never-ending thirst to get better," he said. "It's
like a sport, you have to practice and you have to study."
Alex admitted that even though he's now an established
writer, he still reads screenwriting books, looking for
places where his craft could stand improving. "It's a constant learning process," he said.

The other thing I noticed about Alex is that this learning is not done in isolation: "You need to be constantly
soliciting feedback from colleagues and professionals,"
he told me. During his rise, Alex consistently chose proj-

ects where he'd be forced to show his work to others. While still working as an assistant at NBC, for example, he was writing two pilots: one for VH1 and another with a producer he met at the *National Lampoon*. In both cases, people were waiting to see his scripts—there was no avoiding having them be read and dissected. His *Curb Your Enthusiasm* spec, to name another example, which helped him land his job with Michael Eisner, underwent a lot of scrutiny from Alex's colleagues, at his request. "When I look back now, I'm humiliated that I ever showed it to anyone," Alex recalled. But it was necessary if he was going to get better. "I hope I can look back ten years later and say the same about what I'm writing now."

In Alex, we see exactly the traits that Anders Ericsson defined as crucial for deliberate practice. He stretched his abilities by taking on projects that were beyond his current comfort zone; and not just one at a time, but often up to three or four writing commissions concurrently, all the while holding down a day job! He then obsessively sought feedback, *on everything*—even if, looking back now, he's humiliated at the quality of scripts he was sending out. This is textbook deliberate practice: And it worked. It allowed Alex to acquire career capital in a winner-take-all market that's notoriously reluctant to hand it out.

We see a similar commitment to deliberate practice in Mike Jackson's story. In each stage of his path to becoming a venture capitalist he threw himself into a project beyond his current capabilities and then hustled to make it a success. He took on an ambitious master's thesis that he then translated into leading an even more ambitious international research project. He went from the project into the harsh world of start-ups, where, without outside investment, his ability to pay his rent was dependent on him figuring things out quickly.

Furthermore, at all stages of this path, Mike was not only stretching himself, he was also receiving direct feedback. The work he was leading for the international research project was being prepared for peer review— the epitome of ruthless response. When running his start-up, this feedback took the form of how much money came through the door. If he ran the company poorly, there would be no escaping this fact: His critique would arrive in the form of bankruptcy.

In his current position as a venture capitalist, Mike maintains his dedication to stretching his ability, guided by feedback. His new tool of choice is a spreadsheet, which he uses to track how he spends every hour of every day. "At the beginning of each week I figure out how much time I want to spend on different activities," he explained. "I then track it so I can see how close I came to my targets." On the sample spreadsheet he sent me, he divides his activities into two categories: *hard to change* (i.e., weekly commitments he can't avoid) and *highly changeable* (i.e., self-directed activities that he controls). Here's the amount of time he dedicates to each:

Mike Jackson's Work-Hour Allocation
Hard-to-Change Commitments

Activity	Hours Allocated for the Week
E-mail	7.5
Lunch/Breaks/Other	4
Planning/Organization	1.5
Partner Meeting/Administrative	4
Weekly Fund-raising Meeting	1

Highly Changeable Commitments

Activity	Hours Allocated for the Week
Improving Fund-raising Materials	3
Fund-raising Process	12
Due Diligence Research	3
Deal Flow Sourcing	3
Meetings/Calls with Potential Investors	1
Work with Portfolio Companies	2
Networking/Professional Development	3

Mike's goal with his spreadsheet is to become more "intentional" about how his workday unfolds. "The easiest thing to do is to show up to work in the morning and just respond to e-mail the whole day," he explained. "But that is not the most strategic way to spend your time." Mike now freely admits that he doesn't "do much e-mail." Even after we had been working for a while on the interviews for this book, my scheduling e-mails to Mike only sporadically generated a reply. I eventually figured out that it worked better to call him while he was commuting to his Palo Alto office. On reflection, of course, this makes perfect sense from Mike's perspective. Spending hours every day sorting through non-critical e-mail from authors such as myself or from business students fishing for tips, among other trivialities, would impede his ability to raise money and find good companies— ultimately the job he's judged on. Does he annoy some people because of this lack of availability? Probably. But take my example of eventually being forced to call him during his commute: The important stuff still finds its way to him, but on *his* schedule.

When you look at Mike's spreadsheet, you also notice that he restricts the hours dedicated to required tasks that don't ultimately make him better at what he does (eighteen hours). The majority of his week is instead focused on what matters: raising money, vetting investments, and helping his fund's companies (twenty-seven hours). Without this careful tracking, this ratio would be much different.

This is a great example of deliberate practice at work. "I want to spend time on what's important, instead of what's immediate," Mike explained. At the end of every week he prints his numbers to see how well he achieved this goal, and then uses this feedback to guide himself in the week ahead. The fact that he's been promoted three times in less than three years underscores the effectiveness of this deliberate approach.

The Five Habits of a Craftsman

The stories of Alex Berger and Mike Jackson provide a nice example of deliberate practice in a knowledge-work setting. It can still be difficult, however, to figure out how to apply this strategy in your own working life. Motivated by this reality, I drew from the research literature on deliberate practice, as well as from the stories of craftsman like Alex and Mike, to construct a series of steps for successfully applying this strategy. In this section, I'll detail these steps. There is no magic formula, but deliberate practice is a highly technical process, so I'm hoping that this specificity will help you get started.

Step 1: Decide What Capital Market You're In

For the sake of clarity, I will introduce some new terminology. When you are acquiring career capital in a field, you can imagine that you are acquiring this capital in a specific type of career capital **market**. There are two types of these markets: *winner-take-all* and *auction*. In a winner-take-all market, there is only one type of career capital available, and lots of different people competing for it. Television writing is a winner-take-all market because all that matters is your ability to write good scripts. That is, the only capital type is your script-writing capability.

An auction market, by contrast, is less structured: There are many different types of career capital, and each person might generate a unique collection. The clean-tech space is an auction market. Mike Jackson's capital, for example, included expertise in renewable energy markets and entrepreneurship, but there are a variety of other types of relevant skills that also could have led to a job in this field.

With this in mind, the first task in building a deliberate practice strategy is to figure out what type of career capital market you are competing in. Answering this question might seem obvious, but it's surprisingly easy to get it wrong. In fact, this is how I interpret the beginning of Alex's story. When he arrived in Los Angeles, he treated the entertainment industry as an auction market. By taking a job as a Web editor at the *National Lampoon*, he began to build up a stable of college-aged humor writers. He also filmed a pilot for a low-budget show for the organization. These actions make sense in an auction market where it's important to build up a diverse collection of capital. But the entertainment industry is not an auction market; it's instead winner-take-all. If you want a career in television writing, as Alex discovered, only one thing matters: the quality of your scripts. It took him a year to realize his mistake, but once he did, he left the *Lampoon* to become an assistant to a TV executive so he could better understand the single type of capital of any value to his field. It was only at this point that he began to gain traction in his career.

Mistaking a winner-take-all for an auction market is common. I see it often in an area relevant to my own life: blogging. Here's a typical e-mail from among the many I receive from people asking for advice on growing their own blog audience:

> *"I've finished my first month of posting and am at about three thousand views. The bounce rate, however, is incredibly high, particularly through Digg and Reddit submissions, where it can get close to 90 percent. I'm wondering what next steps you think I should take to bring down the bounce rate?"*

This new blogger was viewing blogging as an auction market. In his conception, there are many different types of capital relevant to your blog—from its format, to its post frequency, to its search-engine optimization, to how easy it is to find it on social networks (this particular blogger invested serious time in submitting every post to as many social networking sites as possible). He viewed the world through statistics and hoped that with the right combination of capital he could get them where he needed them to be to make money. The problem, however, is that blogging in the advice space—where his site existed—is not an auction market, it's winner-take-all. The only capital that matters is whether or not your posts compel the reader.

Some top blogs in this space have notoriously clunky designs, but they all accomplish the same baseline goal: They inspire their readers. When you correctly understand the market where blogging exists, you stop calculating your bounce rate and start focusing instead on saying something people really care about—which is where your energy should be if you want to succeed.

Mike Jackson, by contrast, correctly identified that he was in an auction market. He wasn't sure exactly what he wanted to do, but he knew it would involve the environment, so he set out to gain any capital relevant to this broad topic.

Step 2: Identify Your Capital Type

Once you've identified your market, you must then identify the specific type of capital to pursue. If you're in a winner-take-all market, this is trivial: By definition, there's only one type of capital that matters. For an auction market, however, you have flexibility. A useful heuristic in this situation is to seek *open gates*—opportunities to build capital that are already open to you. For example, Mike Jackson's next step after his degree was to work with a Stanford professor on his environmental-policy research. This decision helped Mike acquire a key type of career capital—a nuanced understanding of international energy markets. At the same time, however, keep in mind that this was also an opportunity that was open to Mike because he was already a Stanford student earning a degree in the field. This made it relatively easy for him to jump into this new role. For someone outside of Stanford, by contrast, being put in charge of such an important project would have been a much less likely proposition.

The advantage of open gates is that they get you farther faster, in terms of career capital acquisition, than starting from scratch. It helps to think about skill acquisition like a freight train: Getting it started requires a huge application of effort, but changing its track once it's moving is easy. In other words, it's hard to start from scratch in a new field. If, for example, Mike had decided to leave Stanford to go work for a private sustainability non-profit, he would have been starting at the ground floor with no particular leg up. By instead leveraging his Stanford education to gain a position with a Stanford professor, he was acquiring valuable capital much sooner.

Step 3: Define "Good"

It's at this point, once you've identified exactly what skill to build, that you can, for guidance, begin to draw from the research on deliberate practice. The first thing this literature tells us is that you need clear goals. If you don't know where you're trying to get to, then it's hard to take effective action. Geoff Colvin, an editor at *Fortune* magazine who wrote a book on deliberate practice,[7] put it this way in an article that appeared in *Fotune*: "[Deliberate practice] requires good goals."[8]

When you ask a musician like Jordan Tice, for example, there's little ambiguity about what getting "good" means to him at that moment. There's always some new, more complicated technique to master. For Alex Berger, the definition of "good" was also clear: his scripts being taken seriously. To give a concrete example, one of the projects he was working on while still an assistant was the development of a spec script to submit to talent agencies. For him, at this early stage of his career capital acquisition, "good" meant having a script good enough to land him an agent. There was no ambiguity about what it meant to succeed at this goal.

Step 4: Stretch and Destroy

Returning to Geoff Colvin, in the article cited above he gives the following warning about deliberate practice:

> *Doing things we know how to do well is enjoyable, and that's exactly the opposite of what deliberate practice demands. . . . Deliberate practice is above all an effort of focus and concentration. That is what makes it "deliberate," as distinct from the mindless playing of scales or hitting of tennis balls that most people engage in.*

If you show up and do what you're told, you will, as Anders Ericsson explained earlier in this chapter, reach an "acceptable level" of ability before plateauing. The good news about deliberate practice is that it will push you past this plateau and into a realm where you have little competition. The bad news is that the reason so few people accomplish this feat is exactly because of the trait Colvin warned us about: *Deliberate practice is often the opposite of enjoyable.*

I like the term "stretch" for describing what deliberate practice feels like, as it matches my own experience with the activity. When I'm learning a new mathematical technique—a classic case of deliberate practice—the uncomfortable sensation in my head is best approximated as a physical strain, as if my neurons are physically re-forming into new configurations. As any mathematician will admit, this stretching feels much different than applying a technique you've already mastered, which can be quite enjoyable. But this stretching, as any mathematician will also admit, is the precondition to getting better.

This is what you should experience in your own pursuit of "good." If you're not uncomfortable, then you're probably stuck at an "acceptable level."

Pushing past what's comfortable, however, is only one part of the deliberate-practice story; the other part is embracing honest feedback—even if it destroys what you thought was good. As Colvin explains in his *Fortune* article, "You may think that your rehearsal of a job interview was flawless, but your opinion isn't what counts." It's so tempting to just assume what you've done is good enough and check it off your to-do list, but it's in honest, sometimes harsh feedback that you learn where to retrain your focus in order to continue to make progress.

Alex Berger, for example, went to elaborate lengths to keep a constant stream of feedback coming. Recall that during his first year of seriously pursuing career capital in television writing, he was working on two pilots: one for VH1 and another with a producer he met at the *National Lampoon*. In both cases, he was working with professionals who wouldn't hesitate to let him know what was working and what was not in his writing. Though he now describes himself as being somewhat "humiliated" by the quality of writing he was putting out for feedback at this stage, he also recognizes that the continuous and harsh feedback he received accelerated the growth of his ability.

· *Step 5: Be Patient*

In his 2007 interview with Charlie Rose, here's how Steve Martin explained his strategy for learning the banjo: "[I thought], if I stay with it, then one day I will have been playing for forty years, and anyone who sticks with something for forty years will be pretty good at it."

To me, this is a phenomenal display of patience. Learning clawhammer banjo is hard, and because of this, Martin was willing to look forty years into the future for the payoff—a recognition of the frustrating months of hard work and mediocre playing ahead. In his memoir, Martin expounds on this idea when he discusses the importance of "diligence" for his success in the entertainment business. What's interesting is that Martin redefines the word so that it's less about paying attention to your main pursuit, and more about your willingness to ignore other pursuits that pop up along the way to distract you. The final step for applying deliberate practice to your working life is to adopt this style of diligence.

The logic works as follows: Acquiring capital can take time. For Alex, it took about two years of serious deliberate practice before his first television script was produced. Mike Jackson was a half decade out of college before cashing in his capital to land a dream job.

This is why Martin's diligence is so important: Without this patient willingness to reject shiny new pursuits, you'll derail your efforts before you acquire the capital you need. I think the image of Martin returning to his banjo, day after day, for forty years, is poignant. It captures well the feel of how career capital is actually acquired: You stretch yourself, day after day, month after month, before finally looking up and realizing, "Hey, I've become pretty good, and people are starting to notice."

Summary of Rule #2

Rule #1 took on the conventional wisdom about how people end up loving what they do. It argued that **the passion hypothesis**, which says that the key to loving your work is to match a job to a pre-existing passion, is bad advice. There's little evidence that most people have pre-existing passions waiting to be discovered, and believing that there's a magical *right* job lurking out there can often lead to chronic unhappiness and confusion when the reality of the working world fails to match this dream.

Rule #2 was the first to tackle the natural follow-up question: *If "follow your passion" is bad advice, what should you do instead?* It contended that the traits that define great work are rare and valuable. If you want these traits in your own life, you need rare and valuable skills to offer in return. I called these rare and valuable skills **career capital**, and noted that the foundation of constructing work you love is acquiring a large store of this capital.

With this in mind, we turned our attention to this process of capital acquisition. I argued that it's important to adopt the **craftsman mindset**, where you focus relentlessly on what value you're offering the world. This stands in stark contrast to the much more common **passion mindset**, which has you focus only on what value the world is offering you.

Even with the craftsman mindset, however, becoming "so good they can't ignore you" is not trivial. To help these efforts I introduced the well-studied concept of **deliberate practice**, an approach to work where you deliberately stretch your abilities beyond where you're comfortable and then receive ruthless feedback on your performance. Musicians, athletes, and chess players know all about deliberate practice. Knowledge workers, however, do not. This is great news for knowledge workers: If you can introduce this strategy into your working life you can vault past your peers in your acquisition of career capital.

RULE #3

Turn Down a Promotion

(Or, the Importance of Control)

Chapter Eight

The Dream-Job Elixir

In which I argue that control over what you do, and how you do it, is one of the most powerful traits you can acquire when creating work you love.

The Mysterious Red Fire Appeal

When Ryan Voiland graduated college in 2000 with an Ivy League diploma in hand, he didn't follow his classmates into the big-city banks or management consultancies. Instead he did something unexpected: He bought farmland. Ryan's acreage is in Granby, Massachusetts, a small town of six thousand in the center of the state, not far south from Amherst. The land quality in Granby is mixed—it's too far east from the Connecticut River to guarantee access to the river valley's best soil—but Ryan still managed to coax a variety of fruits and vegetables out of his plot. He called the fledgling concern Red Fire Farm.

When I arrived in May 2011 to spend a day at Red Fire, Ryan, who is now working with his wife, Sarah, had seventy acres of organic produce under cultivation. The bulk of Red Fire's revenue comes from their Community

Supported Agriculture (CSA) program, in which subscribers pay for a share of the farm's output at the beginning of the growing season and then pick up their produce every week at distribution stands throughout the state. In 2011, the program had around 1,300 CSA subscribers and had started to turn people away—there was more demand than they could meet.

In other words, Red Fire Farm is a success, but this is not what drew me to Granby. I arranged to spend a day with Ryan and Sarah for a more personal reason: I wanted to figure out why their lifestyle was so appealing.

To clarify, I'm not the only one entranced by Red Fire. This is a farm with fans. When Ryan and Sarah arrange special events throughout the year—a dinner to celebrate the summer strawberry harvest, for example, or their fall pumpkin festival—they quickly sell out. During my last visit I overheard a middle-aged woman tell her friend, "I just *love* Ryan and Sarah"—and I'm pretty sure they'd never actually met. The *idea* of Ryan and Sarah, and what their lifestyle represents, was enough to draw her to Granby.

This appeal, of course, goes beyond just Red Fire. The dream of leaving the rat race to start a farm, or otherwise live in harmony with the land, is the perennial fantasy of the cubicle-bound. In recent years, the *New York Times*, for example, has made great sport of telling the story of ex-bankers who head off to Vermont to start farms (stories that usually end with the banker slinking home, mud-stained hat in hand). Something about working outdoors, sun on your back, no computer screen in sight, is undeniably appealing. *But why?*

This question motivated my visit to Red Fire. I was unlikely to move out to the country, but if I could isolate the underlying traits that attracted me to this lifestyle, I reasoned, I could perhaps then integrate some of these traits into my own life in the city. In other words, figuring out this appeal became a key goal in my quest to understand how people end up loving what they do. So I wrote Ryan and Sarah and asked if I could spend a day following them around. Once they agreed, I packed up my notebook, dusted off my work boots, and drove due west out of Boston: I was on a mission to crack the Red Fire Code.

Cracking the Red Fire Code

Not long into my visit, I joined Ryan and Sarah for lunch at their farmhouse. Their kitchen was small but well-used, packed with cookbooks and hand-labeled herb jars. They served bean sandwiches, open face on local nine-grain bread and topped with thick-cut cheddar. As we ate, I asked Ryan how he ended up becoming a full-time farmer. I figured that if I wanted to understand what made his life appealing today, I needed to first understand how he got here.

As you encountered in Rule #1 and #2 of this book,

by this point in my quest I had developed an unconventional theory on how people end up loving what they do. I argued in Rule #1 that "follow your passion" is bad advice, as the vast majority of people don't have preexisting passions waiting to be discovered and matched to a job. In Rule #2, I then countered that people with compelling careers instead start by getting good at something rare and valuable—building what I called "career capital"—and then cashing in this capital for the traits that make great work great. In this understanding, finding the *right work* pales in importance to *working right*. As Ryan told me his story over lunch, I was gratified to realize that his life provides a terrific case study of these ideas in action.

To start, I'll emphasize that Ryan did not *follow* his passion into farming. Instead, like many people who end up loving what they do, he stumbled into his profession, and then found that his passion for the work increased along with his expertise. Ryan grew up in Granby, but is not from a farming family. "Growing up, I had little exposure to professional growing," he explained. In middle school, Ryan was drawn to a universal interest: making extra spending cash. This entrepreneurial streak led him to a series of schemes, from taking on a paper route to collecting cans for the local recycling center. His business breakthrough, however, came when he started collecting wild blueberries and selling them by the carton. "I put up an umbrella next to the road," he told me, "and started my first farm stand." This, he discovered, was a good way to make a buck.

Ryan advanced from wild-picked berries to selling extra produce from his parents' backyard garden. Looking to increase revenue, he then talked his parents into letting him take over their garden. "My dad was more than happy with that arrangement," he recalls. It was here that Ryan decided to get serious about career capital acquisition. "I read everything about growing that I could get my hands on... zillions of different things," he told me. Soon he expanded his parents' garden to cover most of the backyard, bringing in compost by the truckload to increase yield.

By the time Ryan was in high school he was renting ten acres from a local farmer and hiring part-time help during the summer harvest. He took a loan from the Massachusetts Farm Services Agency to finance the purchase of an old tractor and expanded his business beyond his farm stand to also sell at a farmers market and to a small number of wholesale clients. After graduating high school, Ryan headed off to Cornell's agriculture college to further hone his skills with a degree in fruit and vegetable horticulture—returning home on the weekends in order to keep his rented fields healthy.

Here's what struck me about Ryan's story: He didn't just decide one day that he was passionate about produce and then courageously head off into the countryside to start farming. Instead, by the time he made the plunge into full-time farming in 2001, when he bought his first land, he had been painstakingly acquiring relevant career capital for close to a decade. This might be less sexy than the daydream of quitting your day job one day and then waking up to the rooster's crow the next, but it matches what I consistently found when researching the previous two rules: You have to get good before you can expect good work.

As lunch concluded, I had learned the Red Fire history, but I was still unclear on what exactly made its presence so appealing. As we left the kitchen to tour the farm, however, an insight began to develop. I noticed that as Ryan explained his crops, much of his early wariness fell away. Ryan is shy. When he talks in front of crowds, he tends to rush his sentences to completion, as if apologetic for interrupting. But once he got going on his farming strategies, explaining the difference between Merrimack sandy loam and Paxton silt loam, for example, or his new weeding strategy for the carrot beds, his shyness gave way to the enthusiasm of a craftsman who knows what he's doing and has been given the privilege to put this knowledge to work.

I noticed a similar enthusiasm in Sarah when she discussed her efforts to manage the farm's CSA program and public image. When Sarah joined Ryan in Granby in 2007, she was already an advocate for both organic farming and community-supported agriculture. She had studied environmental policy at Vassar, where she'd stumbled on the college's Poughkeepsie Farm Project CSA. Inspired, she started her own small-scale CSA program after graduating, in nearby Stafford Springs, Connecticut. Coming to Red Fire gave Sarah the opportunity to promote these beliefs on a larger scale—a challenge she clearly relishes.

This, I came to realize, is what's so appealing about the Red Fire lifestyle: *control.* Ryan and Sarah invested their (extensive) career capital into gaining control over what they do and how they do it. Their working lives aren't easy—if I learned anything from my visit to Red Fire, it's that farming is a complicated and stressful pursuit—but their lives are their own to direct, and they're good at this. In other words, the Red Fire appeal is not about working outside in the sun—to farmers, I learned, the weather is something to battle, not to enjoy. And it's not about getting away from the computer screen—Ryan spends all winter using Excel spreadsheets to plan his crop beds, while Sarah spends a healthy chunk of each day managing the farm operations on the office computer. It is, instead, autonomy that attracts the Granby groupies: Ryan and Sarah live a meaningful life on their own terms.

As I'll argue next, control isn't just the source of Ryan and Sarah's appeal, but it turns out to be one of the most universally important traits that you can acquire with your career capital—something so powerful and so essential to the quest for work you love that I've taken to calling it the *dream-job elixir.*

The Power of Control

Ryan and Sarah have heaps of control in their working lives, and this is what makes the Red Fire lifestyle so appealing. The appeal of control, however, is not limited to farmers. Decades of scientific research have identified this trait as one of the most important you can pursue in the quest for a happier, more successful, and more meaningful life. Dan Pink's 2009 bestselling book *Drive*, for example, reviews the dizzying array of different ways that control has been found to improve people's lives.[1] As Pink summarizes the literature, more control leads to better grades, better sports performance, better productivity, and more happiness.

In one such study, mentioned in Pink's book, researchers at Cornell followed over three hundred small businesses, half of which focused on giving control to their employees and half of which did not. The control-centric businesses grew at four times the rate of their counterparts. In another study, which I found during my own research, giving autonomy to middle school teachers in a struggling school district not only increased the rate at which the teachers were promoted, but also, to the surprise of the researchers, *reversed* the downward performance trend of their students.[2]

If you want to observe the power of control up close in the workplace, look toward companies embracing a radical new philosophy called Results-Only Work Environment (or, ROWE, for short). In a ROWE company, all that matters is your results. When you show up to work and when you leave, when you take vacations, and how often you check e-mail are all irrelevant. They leave it to the employee to figure out whatever works best for getting the important things done. "No results, no job: It's that simple," as ROWE supporters like to say.

If you read the business case for ROWE, available online, you find example after example of employees liberated by control.[3] At Best Buy's corporate headquarters, for example, the teams that implemented ROWE saw the rate at which people left plummet by up to 90 percent. "I love the ROWE environment.... It makes me feel like I'm in control of my destiny," said one Best Buy employee.

At the Gap's headquarters, employees in a ROWE pilot study found their happiness and performance improved. "I've never seen my employees happier," said one manager. At a non-profit organization in Redlands, California—the first non-profit to embrace ROWE— 80 percent of the employees reported feeling more engaged while over 90 percent thought it made their life better: which is about as close to universal agreement as is possible in a work setting. And these are just a few examples among many.

The more time you spend reading the research literature, the more it becomes clear: **Giving people more control over what they do and how they do it increases their happiness, engagement, and sense**

of fulfillment. It's no wonder, then, that when you flip through your mental Rolodex of dream jobs, control is often at the core of their appeal. Throughout Rule #3, for example, you'll meet people in a variety of different fields who wielded control to create a working life they love. Among them is a freelance computer programmer who skips work to enjoy sunny days, a medical resident who took a two-year leave from his elite residency program to start a company, and a famous entrepreneur who gave away his millions and sold his possessions to embrace an unencumbered, globe-trotting existence. These examples all have great lives, and as you'll learn, they all used control to create them.

To summarize, if your goal is to love what you do, your first step is to acquire career capital. Your next step is to invest this capital in the traits that define great work. Control is one of the most important targets you can choose for this investment. Acquiring control, however, can be complicated. This is why I've dedicated the remainder of Rule #3 to this goal. In the chapters ahead, you'll follow me on my quest to find out more about this fickle trait.

Chapter Nine

The First Control Trap

*In which I introduce **the first control trap**, which warns
that it's dangerous to pursue more control in your working
life before you have career capital to offer in exchange.*

Jane's Adventurous Vision

Jane understands the importance of control. She was a
talented student who earned top-one-percent scores on
her standardized tests and attended a competitive university, but she was also unhappy with following a traditional
path from college and into a steady, well-paying job. Her
vision for her life was more exotic. As an amateur athlete
who once rode a bike across the country for charity and
competed in an Ironman triathlon, she envisioned a more
adventurous future. A copy of the life plan she sent me
includes the goal of circumnavigating the world's oceans
and traveling without motor power across every continent:
"Australia (by unicycle?)...Antarctica (by dog sled?)." The
list also includes more eccentric goals, such as surviving
in the wilderness "with no tools or equipment" for one
month, and learning how to become a fire breather.

To finance this adventurous life, her plan calls, vaguely, for her to "build a set of low-maintenance websites that recurrently earn enough to support the pursuits on this list." Her goal was to get this revenue up to $3,000 a month, which she calculated to be enough to handle her basic expenses. Eventually, she planned to leverage these experiences to "develop a non-profit to develop my vision of health, human potential, and a life well-lived."

At first glance, Jane might remind you of Ryan and Sarah from Red Fire Farm. She recognized that gaining control over her life trumps simply gaining more income or prestige. Like Ryan trading in his diploma for farmland, this realization gave her the courage to step off a safe career path and instead pursue a more compelling existence. But unlike Ryan and Sarah, Jane's plans faltered. Soon after we met, she revealed that her embrace of control had led her to an extreme decision: *dropping out of college.* It didn't take her long to realize that just because you're committed to a certain lifestyle doesn't mean you'll find people who are committed to supporting *you.*

"The current problem is financial independence," she told me. "After quitting college, I started various businesses, and launched freelance and blog projects, but lost motivation to continue before substantial results came." One of these experiments, a blog that she hoped to become the foundation of her empire of recurrent revenue generation, featured only three posts in nine months.

Jane had discovered a hard truth of the real world: It's really hard to convince people to give you money. "I agree that it would be ideal to continue to develop my vision," she admitted. "However, I also need money in order to eat." Without even a college degree to her name, finding this money was proving difficult. A commitment to dogsledding across Antarctica, it turns out, doesn't read well on a résumé.

Control Requires Capital

Control is seductive. As I discovered at Red Fire Farm, this trait defines the type of dream jobs that keeps cubicle dwellers up at night. It was this appeal that convinced Jane to leave her comfortable life as a student and pursue adventure. In doing so, however, she fell into a trap that threatens many in their quest for control:

The First Control Trap

Control that's acquired without career capital is not sustainable.

In Rule #2, I introduced the idea that career capital is the foundation for creating work you love. You must first generate this capital by becoming good at something rare and valuable, I argued, then invest it in the traits that help make great work great. In the last chapter, I argued that control is one of the most valuable traits you can invest in. Jane recognized the second part of this argument: Control is powerful. But she unfortunately skipped the first part—you need something valuable to offer in return for this powerful trait. In other words, she tried to obtain control without any capital to offer in return, and ended up with a mere shadow of real autonomy. Ryan of Red Fire Farm, by contrast, avoided this trap by building up a decade's worth of relevant career capital *before* taking the dive into full-time farming.

This trap might sound familiar, as we saw an example of it earlier in Rule #2, where I told the story of Lisa Feuer. As you'll recall, Feuer gave up her career in marketing and advertising to start a yoga business, even though her only training in yoga was a monthlong certification course. Like Jane, she went after more control *without* the capital to back it up. Also like Jane, this path soon veered in a difficult direction: Within a year, Feuer was on food stamps.

The more I studied examples of control, the more I encountered people who had made these same mistakes. Jane's story, for example, is just one of many from the growing lifestyle-design community. This movement argues that you don't have to live life by other people's rules. It encourages its followers to design their own path through life—preferably one that's exciting and enjoyable to live. It's easy to find examples of this philosophy in action, because many of its disciples blog about their exploits.

At a high level, of course, there's nothing wrong with this philosophy. The author Timothy Ferriss, who coined the term "lifestyle design," is a fantastic example of the good things this approach to life can generate (Ferriss has more than enough career capital to back up his adventurous existence). But if you spend time browsing the blogs of lesser-known lifestyle designers, you'll begin to notice the same red flags again and again: A distressingly large fraction of these contrarians, like Jane, skipped over the part where they build a stable means to support their unconventional lifestyle. They assume that generating the courage to pursue control is what matters, while everything else is just a detail that is easily worked out.

One such blogger I found, to give another example from among many, quit his job at the age of twenty-five, explaining, "I was fed up with living a 'normal' conventional life, working 9–5 for the man [and] having no time and little money to pursue my true passions...so I've embarked on a crusade to show you and the rest of the world how an average Joe...can build a business from scratch to support a life devoted to living 'The Dream.'" The "business" he referenced, as is the case with many lifestyle designers, was his blog about being a lifestyle designer. In other words, his only product was his enthusiasm about not having a "normal" life. It doesn't take an economist to point out there's not much real value lurking there. Or, put into our terminology, enthusiasm alone is not rare and valuable and is therefore not worth much in terms of career capital. This lifestyle designer was investing in a valuable trait but didn't have the means to pay for it.

Not surprisingly, things soon turned bleak on this fellow's blog. After three months of posting several times a week about how to fund an unconventional life through blogging—even though he wasn't making any money himself from his own site—some frustration crept into his writing. In one post, he says, with evident exasperation, "What I noticed is that [readers] come and go. I've put in the hard yards, writing quality posts and finding awesome people...but alas many of [you] just come and go. This is as annoying as trying to fill up a bucket with water that has a bunch of holes in it." He then goes on to detail his ten-point plan for building a more stable audience. The plan includes steps such as "#2. Bring the ENERGY" and "#4. Shower Your Readers with Appreciation," but the list still excludes the most important step of all: giving readers content they're willing to pay for. A few weeks later, the posts on the blog stopped. By the time I found it, there hadn't been a single new post in over four months.

This story provides another clear example of the first control trap: If you embrace control without capital, you're likely to end up like Jane, Lisa, or our poor frustrated lifestyle designer—enjoying all the autonomy you can handle but unable to afford your next meal. This first trap, however, turns out to be only half of the story of why control can be a tricky trait to acquire. As I'll detail in the next chapter, even after you have the capital required to acquire real control, things remain difficult, as it's exactly at this point that people begin to recognize your value and start pushing back to keep you entrenched in a less autonomous path.

Chapter Ten

The Second Control Trap

*In which I introduce **the second control trap**, which warns that once you have enough career capital to acquire more control in your working life, you have become valuable enough to your employer that they will fight your efforts to gain more autonomy.*

Why Lulu Keeps Turning Down Promotions

Lulu Young is a software developer and she loves what she does. She lives in Roslindale, a close-in suburb of Boston, in a beautifully renovated duplex. When I met her there on a rainy spring day in 2011 to talk about work and control, she needed little prompting before diving into one of the more detailed autobiographies I had so far encountered in my quest. I can tell you, for example, that she scored a 5 on her AP chemistry test in high school and that landing her first job involved a chance encounter with an old employer at a Bertucci's in Wellesley Hills. Here's what I wrote in my notes not long into the interview: "This is someone who has put *a lot* of thought into her career."

This thoughtfulness evidently paid off, as Lulu turned out to be one of the more confident and contented subjects I have encountered in my interviews. At the core of this contentment is control. Throughout her career, Lulu repeatedly fought to gain more freedom in her working life, sometimes to the shock or dismay of her employers or friends. "People tell me that I don't do things the way other people do," Lulu said. "But I tell them, 'I'm not other people.'"

She succeeded in these fights, as you'll learn, because she was wary of the first control trap, which was described in the previous chapter. That is, she was careful to ensure she always had enough career capital to back her up before she made a bid for more control. This is a major reason that I want to tell her story: She provides a great example of control done right.

Lulu's first job after graduating Wellesley College with a mathematics degree was at the bottom rung of the software-development career ladder: She was working in Quality Assurance (QA), a fancy term for software tester.

"So your job would be, for example, to put text in bold and then make sure it worked?" I asked her, as she explained this first job. "Whoa, whoa, let's not exaggerate the amount of responsibility they gave me!" she joked in response.

This was not a great job. In fact, this was not even a decent job. It's here that Lulu could have easily fallen into the first control trap: Finding yourself stuck in a boring job is exactly the point where breaking away to pave your own non-conformist path becomes tempting. Instead, she decided to acquire the career capital required to get somewhere better.

Things played out as follows: Lulu began hacking the UNIX operating system that ran the company's software. She eventually taught herself to build scripts that automated the testing, thus saving the company time and money. Her innovations attracted notice, and after a few short years she was promoted to senior QA engineer.

By this point, Lulu had built up a legitimate store of career capital, so she decided to see what it could buy her. To regain some autonomy from a succession of micromanaging bosses who had been tormenting her, she demanded a thirty-hour-a-week schedule so she could pursue a part-time degree in philosophy from Tufts. "I would have asked for less time, but thirty was the minimum for which you could still receive full benefits," she explained. If Lulu had tried this during her first year of employment, her bosses would have laughed and probably offered her instead a "zero-hour-a-week schedule," but by the time she had become a senior engineer and was leading their testing automation efforts, they really couldn't say no.

After she earned her degree, Lulu quit the company and brought her QA automation skills to a nearby start-up that had just been acquired by a major firm. "I had this spacious office with three computer screens," she recalls. "Every week the office manager would come by to take our candy order. You would tell her what candy you wanted, and it would show up on your desk....I had a lot of fun."

After several years, the parent company of the start-up decided to shut down the Boston-area office, so Lulu, who had just bought a house, decided it was time for something different. When she reentered the job market, she generated several offers, including one to manage the QA group for a large company. This would have been a big promotion for Lulu: more money, more power, and more prestige; the next step on a ladder to becoming a hot-shot executive VP.

Lulu turned it down. Instead, she took an offer to work with a seven-person start-up, founded by an old college friend's boyfriend, that had jumped at the chance to acquire someone with such proven skills. "I didn't really understand what they did, and I'm not sure they had it all figured out yet either," she told me. But this is exactly what made it appealing to Lulu: tackling something brand-new, where there wasn't a detailed plan in place already, seemed interesting—a pursuit where she would have a lot of say over what she did and how she did it.

By the time this company was acquired in 2001, Lulu was the head software developer. Given this career capital, when she began to chafe at the new owner's regulations—a dress code, for example, plus insisting that all employees work between the hours of nine and five—she was able to demand (and receive) three months' leave. "There will be no way for you to contact me during this period," she told her new bosses. The leave, it turned out, was also an excuse to train her staff to work without her. Soon after her leave ended, Lulu left and, in a bid for even more control, became a freelance software developer. At this point her skills were so valuable that finding clients was no problem. More importantly, working as a contractor also gave her extreme flexibility in how she did her work. She would travel for three or four weeks at a time when she felt like getting away. "If the weather was nice on a Friday," she told me, "I would just take the day off to go flying" (she obtained her pilot's license around this time). When she started work and when she ended her days were up to her. "A lot of those days I would take a niece or nephew and have fun. I went to the children's museum and zoo probably more than anybody else in the city," she recalls. "They couldn't stop me from doing these things, as I was just a contractor."

I interviewed Lulu early on a weekday afternoon, and the timing didn't seem to matter at all. "Hold on, let me make sure Skype is turned off so no one can bother me," she told me soon after I arrived. Taking an afternoon off on a whim to do an interview is not the type of decision she could have gotten away with if she had followed a traditional career path to become a stock-owning, Porsche-driving, ulcer-suffering VP. But then again, stock-owning, Porsche-driving, ulcer-suffering VPs probably enjoy their lives quite a bit less than Lulu.

Control Generates Resistance

Lulu's story, as I mentioned earlier, is an example of control done right. Like Ryan and Sarah of Red Fire Farms, her career is compelling because she has infused it with control over what she does and how she does it. Also like Ryan and Sarah, she succeeds in this effort where others have failed—for example, Jane from the last chapter—by always making sure she has the career capital needed to obtain this autonomy.

Lurking in this story, however, is a hidden danger. Though Lulu's career was satisfyingly self-directed, the path to acquiring this freedom generated conflict. Almost every time she invested her career capital to obtain the most control, she also encountered resistance. When she leveraged her value to obtain a thirty-hour schedule at her first job, for example, her employer couldn't say no (she was saving them too much money), but they didn't like it. It took nerve on Lulu's part to push through that demand. Similarly, when she turned down a major promotion to take an ill-defined position at a seven-person start-up, people in her life didn't understand.

"You had just bought a house," I reminded her. "To turn down a big important job to go work with an unknown little company, that's a big deal."

"People thought I was nuts," she agreed. Leaving this start-up after it was acquired was similarly difficult. Lulu was hesitant to get into details, but the subtext was that her value was so high at this company that its new owners tried every tactic they could to keep her on board. And finally, her transition to freelance work came with its own difficulties. Her first client really wanted to hire her full-time to work on the project, but she refused. "They really didn't want a contractor," she recalls, "but they didn't have anyone else who could do this type of work, so they eventually had no choice but to agree."

The more I met people who successfully deployed control in their career, the more I heard similar tales of resistance from their employers, friends, and families. Another example is someone I'll call Lewis, who is a resident in a well-known combined plastic surgery program, which is arguably the most competitive medical residency. Three years into his residency, he was starting to chafe under hospital bureaucracy. When I met him for coffee, he gave me a vivid example of the frustrations of life as a modern doctor.

"I once received this patient in the ER who had his chest cut open because he had been stabbed in the heart," he told me. "I'm on the gurney, massaging his heart with my hands as he's brought into the operating room. We get to the room, and obviously this guy needs a blood transfusion because he has a hole in his heart.

" 'Where's the blood?' I ask.

" 'We can't give it to you,' the tech replied. 'You skipped registration when you came in'—remember, I literally had this guy's heart in my hand when we came through the door—and I was thinking, 'You got to be freaking kidding me.' "

That patient died in the OR. He probably would still have died even if he had been given a blood transfusion, but the point is that this was exactly the type of autonomy-demolishing experience that was eating away at Lewis. He craved more control in his life, so he did something unexpected: He took two years off from his residency program to start a company that builds online medical education tools.

When you ask Lewis why he wanted to start a company, he paints a compelling picture. "One thing a lot of people struggle with in my field is that they have a lot of ideas, but don't know how to get them turned into reality." In his vision, he would become a doctor, but also be the cofounder of this company that would continue to run without requiring his day-to-day supervision. As he came up with ideas around medical education, an interest of his, he could then hand them over to the team at the company to be turned into reality.

"Let's say I have this idea for a game that could help premed students learn some sort of new concept," he told me when I asked for an example. "I could turn to my team at the company and say, 'Go make this happen.'" To Lewis, there's a great sense of satisfaction in "creating something that actually works," and this company would provide him that opportunity.

As with Lulu, however, once Lewis had enough medical expertise to successfully raise the funding to begin this company, he had become valuable enough to his employer that they didn't want to let him go. He was the first person in the ten-year history of his combined plastic surgery program to request time off in the middle of his residency. "They were asking me, 'Why would you do this!?'" he recalls. It was not an easy transition to make. When I met Lewis, however, his two-year break was almost up. During this time, his company had progressed from an idea into a well-funded organization with a popular flagship product (a tool that helps med students prepare for their board exams) and a full-time staff that will keep things rolling as he returns to finish his residency. Lewis was clearly happy about his decision to push for something different—but it hadn't been easy.

This is the irony of control. When no one cares what you do with your working life, you probably don't have enough career capital to do anything interesting. But once you do have this capital, as Lulu and Lewis discovered, you've become valuable enough that your employer will resist your efforts. This is what I came to think of as the second control trap:

The Second Control Trap

The point at which you have acquired enough career capital to get meaningful control over your working life is exactly the point when you've become valuable enough to your current employer that they will try to prevent you from making the change.

On reflection, this second trap makes sense. Acquiring more control in your working life is something that benefits *you* but likely has no direct benefit to your employer. Downshifting to a thirty-hour-per-week schedule, for example, provided Lulu freedom from a working environment that had felt increasingly stifling. But from the point of view of her employer, it was simply lost productivity. In other words, in most jobs you should *expect* your employer to resist your move toward more control; they have every incentive to try to convince you to reinvest your career capital back into your career at their company, obtaining more money and prestige instead of more control, and this can be a hard argument to resist.

Courage Revisited

Back in Rule #2, I was dismissive of the "courage culture." This was my term for the growing number of authors and online commentators who promote the idea that the only thing standing between you and a dream job is building the courage to step off the expected path. I argued that it was this courage culture that led Lisa Feuer to quit her corporate job to chase an ill-fated yoga venture. This culture also plays a big role in egging on the less successful members of the lifestyle-design community.

In light of the second control trap, I need to moderate my previous disdain. Courage is *not* irrelevant to creating work you love. Lulu and Lewis, as we now understand, required quite a bit of courage to ignore the resistance generated by this trap. The key, it seems, is to know when the time is right to become courageous in your career decisions. Get this timing right, and a fantastic working life awaits you, but get it wrong by tripping the first control trap in a premature bid for autonomy, and disaster lurks. The fault of the courage culture, therefore, is not its underlying message that courage is good, but its severe underestimation of the complexity involved in deploying this boldness in a useful way.

Imagine, for example, that you come up with an idea for injecting more control into your career. As I argued earlier, this is an idea worth paying attention to because control is so powerful in transforming your working life that I call it the dream-job elixir. Also imagine, however, that as you toy with this idea, people in your life start offering resistance. What's the right thing to do? The two control traps make this a hard question to answer.

It's possible that you don't have enough career capital to back up this bid for more control. That is, you're about to fall into the first control trap. In this case, you should heed the resistance and shelve the idea. At the same time, however, it's possible that you have plenty of career capital, and this resistance is being generated exactly because you're so valuable. That is, you've fallen into the second control trap. In this case, you should ignore the resistance and pursue the idea. This, of course, is the problem with control: Both scenarios feel the same, but the right response is different in each.

By this point in my quest, I've encountered enough stories of control going both right and wrong to know that this conundrum is serious—perhaps one of the single most difficult obstacles facing us in our quest for work we love. The cheery slogans of the courage culture are obviously too crude to guide us through this tricky territory. We need a more nuanced heuristic, something that could make clear exactly what brand of control trap you're facing. As you'll learn next, I ended up discovering this solution in the habits of an iconoclastic entrepreneur, someone who has elevated living his life by his own rules to an art form.

Chapter Eleven

Avoiding the Control Traps

*In which I explain the **law of financial viability**, which says you should only pursue a bid for more control if you have evidence that it's something that people are willing to pay you for.*

Derek Sivers Is a Control Freak

Not long into his 2010 TED talk on creativity and leadership, Derek Sivers plays a video clip of a crowd at an outdoor concert. A young man without a shirt starts dancing by himself. The audience members seated nearby look on curiously.

"A leader needs the guts to stand alone and look ridiculous," Derek says. Soon, however, a second young man joins the first and starts dancing.

"Now comes the first follower with a crucial role ... the first follower transforms the lone nut into a leader." As the video continues, a few more dancers join the group. Then several more. Around the two-minute mark, the dancers have grown into a crowd.

"And ladies and gentlemen, that's how a movement is made."[1]

The TED audience gives Derek a standing ovation. He bows, then does a little dance himself on stage.

No one can accuse Derek Sivers of being a conformist. During his career, he has repeatedly played the role of the first dancer. He starts with a risky move, designed to maximize his control over what he does and how he does it. By doing so, he's at risk of looking like the "lone nut" dancing alone. Throughout Derek's career, however, there always ended up being a second dancer who validated his decision, and then eventually a crowd arrived, defining the move as successful.

His first risky move occurred in 1992 when he quit a good job at Warner Bros. to pursue music full-time. He played guitar and toured with the Japanese musician and producer Ryuichi Sakamoto, and by all accounts was pretty good at it. His next big move was in 1997, when he started CD Baby, a company that helped independent artists sell their CDs online. In an age before iTunes, this company filled a crucial need for independent musicians, and the company grew. In 2008, he sold it to Disc Makers for $22 million.

At this point in his career, conventional wisdom dictated that Derek should move to a large house outside of San Francisco and become an angel investor. But Derek was never interested in conventional wisdom. Instead, he put all of the proceeds from the sale into a charitable trust to support music education, living off the smallest possible amount of interest allowed by law. He then sold his possessions and began traveling the world in search of an interesting place to live. When I spoke with him, he was in Singapore. "I love that the country has so little gravity, it doesn't try to hold you here, it's instead a base from which you can go explore," he said. When I asked him why he's living overseas, he replied, "I follow a rule with my life that if something is scary, do it. I've lived everywhere in America, and for me, a big scary thing was living outside the country."

After taking time off to read, learn Mandarin, and travel the world, Derek has recently turned his sights on a new company: MuckWork. This service allows musicians to outsource boring tasks so they can spend more time on the creative things that matter. He started the company because he thought the idea sounded fun.

Here's what interests me about Derek: He loves control. His whole career has been about making big moves, often in the face of resistance, to gain more control over what he does and how he does it. And not only does he love control, but he's fantastically successful at achieving it. This is why I got him on the phone from Singapore: I wanted to find out *how* he achieved this feat. In more detail, I asked what criteria he uses to decide which projects to pursue and which to abandon—in essence, I wanted his map for navigating the control traps described in the last two chapters.

Fortunately for us, he had a simple but surprisingly effective answer to my question....

The Law of Financial Viability

When I explained what I was after, Derek got it right away.

"You mean, the type of mental algorithm that prevents the lawyer, who has had this successful career for twenty years, from suddenly saying, 'You know, I love massages, I'm going to become a masseuse'?" he asked.

"That's it," I replied.

Derek thought for a moment.

"I have this principle about money that overrides my other life rules," he said. **"Do what people are willing to pay for."**

Derek made it clear that this is different from pursuing money for the sake of having money. Remember, this is someone who gave away $22 million and sold his possessions after his company was acquired. Instead, as he explained: "Money is a neutral indicator of value. By aiming to make money, you're aiming to be valuable."

He also emphasized that hobbies are clearly exempt from this rule. "If I want to learn to scuba dive, for example, because I think it's fun, and people won't pay me to do that, I don't care, I'm going to do it anyway," he said. But when it comes to decisions affecting your core career, money remains an effective judge of value. "If you're struggling to raise money for an idea, or are thinking that you will support your idea with unrelated work, then you need to rethink the idea."

At first encounter, Derek's career, which orbits around creative pursuits, might seem divorced from matters as prosaic and crass as money. But when he renarrated his path from the perspective of this mental algorithm, it suddenly made more sense.

His first big move, for example, was to become a professional musician in 1992. As Derek explained to me, he started by pursuing music at night and on the weekend. "I didn't quit my day job until I was making more money with my music."

His second big move was to start CD Baby. Again, he didn't turn his attention full-time to this pursuit until after he had built up a profitable client base. "People ask me how I funded my business," he said. "I tell them first I sold one CD, which gave me enough money to sell two." It grew from there.

In hindsight, Derek's bids for control remain big and non-conformist, but given his mental algorithm on only doing what people are paying for, they now also seem much less risky. This idea is powerful enough that I should give it its own official-sounding title:

The Law of Financial Viability

When deciding whether to follow an appealing pursuit that will introduce more control into your work life, seek evidence of whether people are willing to pay for it. If you find this evidence, continue. If not, move on.

When I began reflecting on this law, I saw that it applied again and again to examples of people successfully acquiring more control in their careers. To understand this, notice that the definition of "willing to pay" varies. In some cases, it literally means customers paying you money for a product or a service. But it can also mean getting approved for a loan, receiving an outside investment, or, more commonly, convincing an employer to either hire you or keep writing you paychecks. Once you adopt this flexible definition of "pay for it," this law starts popping up all over.

Consider, for example, Ryan Voiland from Red Fire Farm. Many well-educated city dwellers, fed up with urban chaos, buy some farmland and try to make a living working with their hands. Most fail. What makes Ryan different is that he made sure people were willing to pay him to farm before he tried it. In more detail, because he wasn't a rich ex-banker, buying his first property required a loan from the Massachusetts Farm Services Agency—and the FSA does not give away its money easily. You have to submit a detailed business plan that convinces them that you'll actually make money with your farm. With ten years of experience on his side, Ryan was able to make this argument.

Lulu provides another good example of this law in action. Here, the definition of "willing to pay" concerned her paycheck. She judged her moves toward more autonomy by whether or not someone would hire her or keep paying her while she made them. Her first big move, for example, was to drop to a thirty-hour-per-week schedule. She knew she had enough capital to support this change because her employer said yes. In later jobs, when she negotiated a three-month leave or insisted on working freelance with an open schedule, these were also bids for more control that were validated by the fact that her employers accepted them. If she had had less career capital they would have had no problem telling her good-bye.

On the flip side, when you look at stories of people who were *unsuccessful* in adding more control to their careers, you often find that this law has been ignored. Remember Jane from earlier in Rule #3: She dropped out of college with the vague idea that some sort of online business would support a lifestyle of adventure. If she had met Derek Sivers, she would have delayed this move until she had real evidence that she could make money online. In this case, the law would have served its purpose well, as a simple experiment would have likely revealed that passive-income websites are more myth than reality, and thus prevented her rash abandonment of her education. This doesn't mean that Jane would have had to resign herself to a life of boring work. On the contrary, the law could have provided her structure to keep exploring variations on her adventurous life vision until she could find one to pursue that would actually yield results.

Summary of Rule #3

Rules #1 and #2 laid the foundation for my new thinking on how people end up loving what they do. Rule #1 dismissed the **passion hypothesis**, which says that you have to first figure out your true calling and then find a job to match. Rule #2 replaced this idea with **career capital theory**, which argues that the traits that define great work are rare and valuable, and if you want these in your working life, you must first build up rare and valuable skills to offer in return. I call these skills "career capital," and in Rule #2 I dived into the details of how to acquire it.

The obvious next question is how to invest this capital once you have it. Rule #3 explored one answer to this question by arguing that gaining **control** over what you do and how you do it is incredibly important. This trait shows up so often in the lives of people who love what they do that I've taken to calling it the dream-job elixir.

Investing your capital in control, however, turns out to be tricky. There are two traps that commonly snare people in their pursuit of this trait. **The first control trap** notes that it's dangerous to try to gain more control without enough capital to back it up.

The second control trap notes that once you have the capital to back up a bid for more control, you're still not out of the woods. This capital makes you valuable enough to your employer that they will likely now fight to keep you on a more traditional path. They realize that gaining more control is good for you but not for their bottom line.

The control traps put you in a difficult situation. Let's say you have an idea for pursuing more control in your career and you're encountering resistance. How can you tell if this resistance is useful (for example, it's helping you avoid the first control trap) or something to ignore (for example, it's the result of the second control trap)?

To help navigate this control conundrum, I turned to Derek Sivers. Derek is a successful entrepreneur who has lived a life dedicated to control. I asked him his advice for sifting through potential control-boosting pursuits and he responded with a simple rule: "Do what people are willing to pay for." This isn't about making money (Derek, for example, is more or less indifferent to money, having given away to charity the millions he made from selling his first company). Instead, it's about using money as a "neutral indicator of value"—a way of determining whether or not you have enough career capital to succeed with a pursuit. I called this **the law of financial viability**, and concluded that it's a critical tool for navigating your own acquisition of control. This holds whether you are pondering an entrepreneurial venture or a new role within an established company. Unless people are willing to pay you, it's not an idea you're ready to go after.

Think Small, Act Big

(Or, the Importance of Mission)

Chapter Twelve

The Meaningful Life of Pardis Sabeti

*In which I argue that a unifying **mission** to your working life can be a source of great satisfaction.*

The Happy Professor

Harvard's state-of-the-art Northwest Science Building is found at 52 Oxford Street in Cambridge, Massachusetts, a ten-minute walk from the tourists packing the university's famed central yard. It's part of a complex of hulking brick-and-glass laboratories that form the new heart of Harvard's fabled research engine. Inside, the Northwest looks like a Hollywood vision of a science lab. The hallways defining the perimeter of each floor are polished concrete and lit dimly in the style of television crime procedurals.

Inside the hallways, in the center of the building, are the wetlabs, with graduate students manipulating pipettes visible through windowed steel doors. On the other side of the hallway are the professors' offices, defined by floor-to-ceiling glass partitions. It was one of these offices in particular that drew me to the Northwest on a sunny June afternoon—the office of Pardis Sabeti, a thirty-five-year-old professor of evolutionary biology who had mastered one of the more elusive but powerful strategies in the quest for work you love.

One of the first things you'll notice if you spend time around Pardis is that she enjoys her life. Biology, like any high-stakes academic field, is demanding. Because of this it has a reputation for turning young professors into curmudgeons who adopt a masochistic brand of worka-holism, in which relaxation becomes a sign of failure and the accomplishments of peers become tragedies. This can be a bleak existence. Pardis, for her part, has avoided this fate.

Not five minutes into my visit, for example, a young grad student, one of ten people Pardis employs in her eponymous Sabeti Lab, pokes his head into the office.

"We're heading down to volleyball practice," he says, referencing the lab's team, which evidently takes itself seriously. She promises to join them as soon as our inter-view ends.

Volleyball is not Pardis's only hobby. In a corner of her office she keeps an acoustic guitar that serves as more than decoration: Pardis plays in a band called Thousand Days, which is well known in Boston music circles. In 2008, PBS featured the band in a *Nova* special called *Researchers Who Rock*.

Pardis's energy for these activities is a side effect of

her enthusiasm for her work. The bulk of her research focuses on Africa, with studies ongoing in Senegal, Sierra Leone, and most of all, Nigeria. To Pardis, this work is about more than just the accumulation of publications and grant money. At one point in our conversation, for example, she pulls out her laptop: "You have to see this video of me and my girls," she says, loading up a You-Tube clip of Pardis, guitar in hand, leading a group of four African women in a song. The video was shot outdoors in Nigeria. Palm trees provide the backdrop. The women, I learn, work in a clinic supported by the Sabeti Lab. "These women deal with people who die in devastating ways every day," she says to no one in particular while the video plays. On screen, everyone is smiling while Pardis leads them, with mixed success, through the verses. "I love going there," she adds. "Nigeria is my African home."

It's clear that Pardis has avoided the grinding cynicism that traps so many young academics, and has instead built an engaging life ("It's not always easy," she once said in an interview, "but I truly love what I do"[1]). *But how did she pull off this feat?* As I spent time with Pardis, I recognized that **her happiness comes from the fact that she built her career on a clear and compelling *mission*** —something that not only gives meaning to her work but provides the energy needed to embrace life beyond the lab. In the overachieving style typical of Harvard, Pardis's mission is by no means subtle: Her goal, put simply, is to rid the world of its most ancient and deadly diseases.

Pardis's Mission

As a graduate student, Pardis stumbled into the emerging field of computational genetics—the use of computers to help understand DNA sequences. She developed an algorithm that sifts through databases of human genetic information looking for traces of an elusive target: ongoing human evolution. To the general public, the idea that humans are still evolving can be surprising, but among evolutionary biologists it's taken for granted. (One of the classic examples of recent human evolution is lactose tolerance—the ability to digest milk into adulthood—a trait that didn't start spreading through the human population until we domesticated milk-producing animals.)

Pardis's algorithm uses statistical techniques to hunt down patterns of gene migration that match what you would expect from selective pressure—for example, a mutation that popped up recently in human development but has since spread quickly among a population. The algorithm, in other words, searches blindly, turning up "candidate" genes that look like they're the result of natural selection, but leaving it up to the researcher to figure out why natural selection deemed the gene useful.

Pardis uses the algorithm to search for recently evolved genes that provide disease resistance. Her logic is that if she can find these genes and understand how they work, biomedical researchers might be able to mimic their benefit in a treatment. It makes sense, of course, that disease-resistance genes would be among the candidates turned up by Pardis's algorithm, as they provide a classic example of natural selection in action. If a deadly virus has been killing off humans in a population for a long time, biologists would say that this population is under "selective pressure." If a lucky few members of the group then happen to evolve a resistance to the disease, this pressure ensures that the new gene will spread quickly (people with the new gene die less frequently than those without it). This rapid spread of a new gene is exactly the type of signature Pardis's algorithm has been tuned to detect.

Pardis's first big discovery was a gene that provides resistance to Lhassa fever, one of the oldest and most deadly diseases of the African continent, responsible for tens of thousands of deaths each year. ("People don't just die with this disease," she emphasized, "they die extreme deaths.") She has since added malaria and the bubonic plague to the list of "ancient scourges" that she's tackling with her computational strategy.

Pardis's career is driven by a clear mission: to use new technology to fight old diseases. This research is clearly important—an observation emphasized by the fact that she's received seven-figure grants for her work from both the Bill and Melinda Gates Foundation and the NIH. Later in this book, we'll dive into the details of how she found this focus, but what's important to note now is that her mission provides her a sense of purpose and energy, traits that have helped her avoid becoming a cynical academic and instead embrace her work with enthusiasm. Her mission is the foundation on which she builds love for what she does, and therefore it's a career strategy we need to better understand.

The Power of Mission

To have a mission is to have a unifying focus for your career. It's more general than a specific job and can span multiple positions. It provides an answer to the question, What should I do with my life? Missions are powerful because they focus your energy toward a useful goal, and this in turn maximizes your impact on your world—a crucial factor in loving what you do. People who feel like their careers truly matter are more satisfied with their working lives, and they're also more resistant to the strain of hard work. Staying up late to save your corporate litigation client a few extra million dollars can be draining, but staying up late to help cure an ancient disease can leave you more energized than when you started—perhaps even providing the extra enthusiasm needed to start a lab volleyball team or tour with a rock band.

I was drawn to Pardis Sabeti because her career is driven by a mission and she's reaped happiness in return.

After meeting her, I went searching for other people who leveraged this trait to create work they love. This search led me to a young archaeologist whose mission to popularize his field led to his own television series on the Discovery Channel, and to a bored programmer who systematically studied marketing to devise a mission that injected excitement back into his working life. In all three cases, I tried to decode exactly how these individuals found and then successfully deployed their missions. In short, I wanted an answer to an important question: *How do you make mission a reality in your working life?*

The answers I found are complicated. To better understand this complexity, let's put the topic back into the broader context of the book. In the preceding rules, I have argued that "follow your passion" is bad advice, as most people aren't born with pre-existing passions waiting to be discovered. If your goal is to love what you do, you must first build up "career capital" by mastering rare and valuable skills, and then cash in this capital for the traits that define great work. As I'll explain, mission is one of these desirable traits, and like any such desirable trait, it too requires that you first build career capital—a mission launched without this expertise is likely doomed to sputter and die.

But capital alone is not enough to make a mission a reality. Plenty of people are good at what they do but haven't reoriented their career in a compelling direction.

Accordingly, I will go on to explore a pair of advanced tactics that also play an important role in making the leap from a good idea for a mission to actually making that mission a reality. In the chapters ahead, you'll learn the value of systematically experimenting with different proto-missions to seek out a direction worth pursuing. You'll also learn the necessity of deploying a marketing mindset in the search for your focus. In other words, missions are a powerful trait to introduce into your working life, but they're also fickle, requiring careful coaxing to make them a reality.

This subtlety probably explains why so many people lack an organizing focus to their careers, even though such focus is widely admired: Missions are hard. By this point in my quest, however, I had become comfortable with "hard," and I hope that if you've made it this far in the book, you have gained this comfort as well. Hardness scares off the daydreamers and the timid, leaving more opportunity for those like us who are willing to take the time to carefully work out the best path forward and then confidently take action.

Chapter Thirteen

Missions Require Capital

In which I argue that a mission chosen before you have
relevant career capital is not likely to be sustainable.

Mission Failure

When Sarah wrote me, she was stuck. She had recently
quit her job as a newspaper editor to attend graduate
school to study cognitive science. Sarah had considered
grad school right out of college, but at the time, she
worried that she didn't have the right skills. With age,
however, came more confidence, and after she signed
up for and then aced an artificial-intelligence course that
would have "scared a younger version of myself," Sarah
decided to take the plunge and become a full-time doc-
toral candidate.

Then the trouble started. Not long into her new student career Sarah became paralyzed by her work's lack
of an organizing mission. "I feel I have too many interests," she told me. "I can't decide if I want to do theoretical work or something more applied, or which would
be more useful. Even more threatening, I believe all the

other researchers to be geniuses.... What would you do if you were in my shoes?"

Sarah's story reminded me of Jane, whom I introduced in Rule #3. As you might recall, Jane dropped out of college to "[start] a non-profit to develop my vision of health, human potential, and a life well-lived." This mission, unfortunately, ran into a harsh financial reality when Jane failed to raise money to support her vague vision. When I met her, she was soliciting advice about finding a normal job, a task that was proving difficult because she lacked a degree.

Both Sarah and Jane recognized the power of mission, but struggled to deploy the trait in their own working lives. Sarah desperately wanted a Pardis Sabeti style of life-transforming research focus, yet her failure to immediately identify such a focus led her to rethink graduate school. Jane, on the other hand, slapped together something vague (a non-profit that would "develop my vision of . . . a life well-lived") and then hoped the details would work themselves out once she got started. Jane fared no better than Sarah: The details, it turned out, did not work themselves out, leaving Jane penniless and still without a college degree.

I tell these stories because they emphasize an important point: Missions are tricky. As Sarah and Jane learned, just because you really want to organize your work around a mission doesn't mean that you can easily make it happen. After my visit to Harvard, I realized that if I was going to deploy this trait in my own career, I needed to better understand this trickiness. That is, I needed to figure out what Pardis did differently than Sarah and Jane. The answer I eventually found came from an unexpected place: the attempts to explain a puzzling phenomenon.

The Baffling Popularity of Randomized Linear Network Coding

As I write this chapter, I'm attending a computer science conference in San Jose, California. Earlier today, something interesting happened. I attended a session in which four different professors from four different universities presented their latest research. Surprisingly, all four presentations tackled the same narrow problem—*information dissemination in networks*—using the same narrow technique—*randomized linear network coding*. It was as if my research community woke up one morning and collectively and spontaneously decided to tackle the same esoteric problem.

This example of joint discovery surprised me, but it would not have surprised the science writer Steven Johnson. In his engaging 2010 book, *Where Good Ideas Come From*, Johnson explains that such "multiples" are frequent in the history of science.[1] Consider the discovery of sunspots in 1611: As Johnson notes, four scientists, from four different countries, all identified the phenomenon during that same year. The first electrical battery? Invented twice in the mid-eighteenth century. Oxygen? Isolated independently in 1772 and 1774. In one study cited by Johnson, researchers from Columbia University found just shy of 150 different examples of prominent scientific breakthroughs made by multiple researchers at near the same time.

These examples of simultaneous discovery, though interesting, might seem tangential to our interest in career mission. I ask, however, that you stick with me, as the explanation for this phenomenon is the first link in a chain of logic that helped me decode what Pardis did differently than Sarah and Jane.

Big ideas, Johnson explained, are almost always discovered in the "adjacent possible," a term borrowed from the complex-system biologist Stuart Kauffman, who used it to describe the spontaneous formation of complex chemical structures from simpler structures. Given a soup of chemical components sloshing and mixing together, noted Kauffman, lots of new chemicals will form. Not every new chemical, however, is equally likely. The new chemicals you'll find are those that can be made by combining the structures already in the soup. That is, the new chemicals are in the space of the *adjacent possible* defined by the current structures.

When Johnson adopted the term, he shifted it from complex chemicals to cultural and scientific innovations. "We take the ideas we've inherited or that we've stumbled across, and we jigger them together into some new shape," he explained. The next big ideas in any field are found right beyond the current cutting edge, in the adjacent space that contains the possible new combinations of existing ideas. The reason important discoveries often happen multiple times, therefore, is that they only become possible once they enter the adjacent possible, at which point anyone surveying this space—that is, those who are the current cutting edge—will notice the same innovations waiting to happen.

The isolation of oxygen as a component of air, to name one of Johnson's examples of a multiple discovery, wasn't possible until two things happened: First, scientists began to think about air as a substance containing elements, not just a void; and second, sensitive scales, a key tool in the needed experiments, became available. Once these two developments occurred, the isolation of oxygen became a big fat target in the newly defined adjacent possible—visible to anyone who happened to be looking in that direction. Two scientists—Carl Wilhelm Scheele and Joseph Priestley—*were* looking in this direction, and therefore both went on to conduct the necessary experiments independently but at nearly the same time.

The adjacent possible also explains my earlier example of four researchers tackling the same obscure problem with the same obscure technique at the conference I attended. The specific technique applied in this case—a technique called randomized linear network coding—came to the attention of the computer scientists I work with only over the last two years, as researchers who study a related topic began to apply it successfully to thorny problems. The scientists who ended up presenting papers on this technique at my conference had all noticed its potential around the same time. Put in Johnson's terms, this technique redefined the cutting edge in my corner of the academic world, and therefore it also redefined the adjacent possible, and in this new configuration the information dissemination problem, like the discovery of oxygen many centuries earlier, suddenly loomed as a big target waiting to be tackled.

We like to think of innovation as striking us in a stunning eureka moment, where you all at once change the way people see the world, leaping far ahead of our current understanding. I'm arguing that in reality, innovation is more systematic. We grind away to expand the cutting edge, opening up new problems in the adjacent possible to tackle and therefore expand the cutting edge some more, opening up more new problems, and so on. "The truth," Johnson explains, "is that technological (and scientific) advances rarely break out of the adjacent possible."

As I mentioned, understanding the adjacent possible and its role in innovation is the first link in a chain of argument that explains how to identify a good career mission. In the next section, I'll forge the second link, which connects the world of scientific breakthroughs to the world of work.

The Capital-Driven Mission

Scientific breakthroughs, as we just learned, require that you first get to the cutting edge of your field. Only then can you see the adjacent possible beyond, the space where innovative ideas are almost always discovered. Here's the leap I made as I pondered Pardis Sabeti around the same time I was pondering Johnson's theory of innovation: **A good career mission is similar to a scientific breakthrough—it's an innovation waiting to be discovered in the adjacent possible of your field**. If you want to identify a mission for your working life, therefore, you must first get to the cutting edge—the only place where these missions become visible.

This insight explains Sarah's struggles: She was trying to find a mission *before* she got to the cutting edge (she was still in her first two years as a graduate student when she began to panic about her lack of focus). From her vantage point as a new graduate student, she was much too far from the cutting edge to have any hope of surveying the adjacent possible, and if she can't see the adjacent possible, she's not likely to identify a compelling new direction for her work. According to Johnson's theory, Sarah would have been better served by first mastering a promising niche—a task that may take years—and only then turning her attention to seeking a mission.

This distance from the adjacent possible also tripped up Jane. She wanted to start a transformative non-profit that changed the way people live their lives. A successful non-profit, however, needs a specific philosophy with strong evidence for its effectiveness. Jane didn't have such a philosophy. To find one, she would have needed a nice view of the adjacent possible in her corner of the non-profit sector, and this would have required that she first get to the cutting edge of efforts to better people's lives—a process that, as with Sarah, requires patience and perhaps years of work. Jane was trying to identify a mission before she got to the cutting edge and she predictably didn't come up with anything that could turn people's heads.

In hindsight, these observations are obvious. If life-transforming missions could be found with just a little navel-gazing and an optimistic attitude, changing the world would be commonplace. But it's not commonplace; it's instead quite rare. This rareness, we now understand, is because these breakthroughs require that you first get to the cutting edge, and this is hard—the type of hardness that most of us try to avoid in our working lives.

The alert reader will notice that this talk of "getting to the cutting edge" echoes the idea of *career capital*, which was introduced back in Rule #2. As you'll recall, career capital is my term for rare and valuable skills. It is, I argued, your main bargaining chip in creating work you love: Most people who love their work got where they are by first building up career capital and then cashing it in for the types of traits that define great work. Getting to the cutting edge of a field can be understood in these terms: This process builds up rare and valuable skills and therefore builds up your store of career capital. Similarly, identifying a compelling mission once you get to the cutting edge can be seen as investing your career capital to acquire a desirable trait in your career. In other words, mission is yet another example of career capital theory in action. If you want a mission, you need to first acquire capital. If you skip this step, you might end up like Sarah and Jane: with lots of enthusiasm but very little to show for it.

Not surprisingly, when we return to the story of Pardis Sabeti, we find that her path to a mission provides a nice example of this career capital perspective translated into practice.

Pardis's Patience

"I think you do need passion to be happy," Pardis Sabeti told me. At first this sounds like she's supporting the *passion hypothesis* that I debunked in Rule #1. But then she elaborated: "It's just that we don't know what that passion is. If you ask someone, they'll tell you what they think they're passionate about, but they probably have it wrong." In other words, she believes that having passion for your work is vital, but she also believes that it's a fool's errand to try to figure out in advance what work will lead to this passion.

When you hear Pardis's story, the origin of this philosophy becomes clear. "In high school, I was obsessed with math," she told me. Then she had a biology teacher whom she loved, which made her think that biology might be for her. When she arrived at MIT, she was forced to choose between math and bio. "It turns out that the MIT bio department has an unbelievable emphasis on teaching," she explained. "So I majored in bio." With a bio major came a new plan: She decided she was destined to become a doctor. "I perceived myself as someone who cared about people. I wanted to practice medicine."

Pardis did very well at MIT, won a Rhodes Scholarship, and used it to go earn her PhD at Oxford. She focused on biological anthropology, a typically archaic Oxfordian name for a field most would simply call genetics.

It was at Oxford that Pardis decided that Africa and infectious diseases were also a potentially interesting topic to study. If you're keeping count, this was the third field that at some point in her student career attracted her—the full list now contains math, medicine, and infectious disease. This is why she's wary of the strategy of trying to identify your one true calling in advance—in her experience, lots of different things can, at different times, seem compelling.

Given her new interest in Africa, Pardis joined a research group using genetic analysis to help African-Americans trace their genealogy back to regions of Africa. After a year or so, Pardis decided to switch labs, and she moved into another, suggested by a friend. This lab was tackling the genetics of malaria.

After Oxford, Pardis returned to Harvard Medical School to earn her MD—amazingly, even as she was finishing up a PhD in genetics, she wasn't ready yet to abandon her earlier premonition that she was somehow meant to be a doctor. The result was that she became a young med student finishing a PhD thesis during her spare time. "If you want to write a thing about having a quality enjoyable life, don't ask me about my time at Harvard," she warned. "Harvard was a tough time."

Pardis finished her dissertation and became a post-doctoral fellow, continuing to juggle this work with the end of her MD program, taking the subway back and forth between Harvard and MIT, where she was now working at the Broad Institute with the famed geneticist Eric Lander. It was during this period that her ideas about using statistical analysis to find evidence of recent human evolution begin to yield results, culminating in the 2002 publication of a major paper in *Nature* with the innocuous title: "Detecting recent positive selection in the human genome from haplotype structure."[2]

According to Google Scholar, the work has been cited over 720 times since its publication. "People started treating me differently after that paper," Pardis says. "That's when the faculty offers started coming in." Though she finished her MD somewhere in this period, it was not until this point that her mission finally became clear: Becoming a clinical doctor didn't make sense; she was going to build a research career focused on her use of computational genetics to combat ancient diseases. Pardis took a professorship at Harvard, finally ready to commit to a single focus in her working life.

What struck me about Pardis's story is how remarkably late it was in her training before she identified the mission that now defines her career. This lateness is best represented by her decision to still attend—*and finish!*—medical school even though she was working on PhD research that was starting to attract notice. These are not the actions of someone who is certain of her destiny from day one. This certainty didn't come until later, around the time of her *Nature* publication, when Pardis had finally developed her computational genetics ideas to the point where their usefulness and novelty were obvious.

To use my terminology, this long period of training, starting with her undergraduate biology classes and continuing through her PhD and then postdoctoral work at the Broad Institute, was when she was building up her stores of career capital. When she took a professorship at

Harvard, she was finally ready to cash in this capital to obtain the mission-driven career she enjoys today.

Rule #4 is entitled "Think Small, Act Big." It's in this understanding of career capital and its role in mission that we get our explanation for this title. Advancing to the cutting edge in a field is an act of "small" thinking, requiring you to focus on a narrow collection of subjects for a potentially long time. Once you get to the cutting edge, however, and discover a mission in the adjacent possible, you must go after it with zeal: a "big" action.

Pardis Sabeti thought small by focusing patiently for years on a narrow niche (the genetics of diseases in Africa), but then acting big once she acquired enough capital to identify a mission (using computational genetics to help understand and fight ancient diseases). Sarah and Jane, by contrast, reversed this order. They started by thinking big, looking for a world-changing mission, but without capital they could only match this big thinking with small, ineffectual acts. The art of mission, we can conclude, asks us to suppress the most grandiose of our work instincts and instead adopt the patience—the style of patience observed with Pardis Sabeti—required to get this ordering correct.

Chapter Fourteen

Missions Require Little Bets

*In which I argue that great missions are transformed
into great successes as the result of using small and
achievable projects—**little bets**—to explore the concrete
possibilities surrounding a compelling idea.*

Leaping the Gap Between Idea and Practice

My time with Pardis Sabeti convinced me that career
capital is necessary to identify a good mission. But even
as this understanding solidified, a nagging thought kept
spoiling my intellectual satisfaction: *Why don't I have a
personal mission-driven career?*

When I met Pardis, I had a PhD in computer science
from MIT and close to two dozen peer-reviewed publications to my name. I'd given talks on my work all over the
world, from Rio to Bologna to Zurich. In other words, I
had accumulated career capital, and this capital allowed
me to identify many potential missions relevant to my
skills. I even had a written record of these brainstorms,
as I always keep an idea notebook with me. On March
13, 2011, for example, I recorded the possibility of focus-

ing my career on a new style of distributed algorithm theory that was just emerging—the study of algorithms in communication graphs with unrestrained topology changes. I could, I noted, immerse myself in its development much in the same way the early proponents of chaos theory did in their field back in the early 1980s.

But this brings me back to my nagging question. I had notebooks filled with potential missions, yet I had resisted devoting myself to any one in particular. And I'm not alone in this reluctance to act. *Many* people have lots of career capital, and can therefore identify a variety of different potential missions for their work, but *few* actually build their career around such missions. It seems, therefore, that there's more to this career tactic than simply getting to the cutting edge. Once you have the capital required to identify a mission, you must still figure out how to put the mission into practice. If you don't have a trusted strategy for making this leap from idea to execution, then like me and so many others, you'll probably avoid the leap altogether.

This chapter is the first of two that investigate people who have successfully made this leap. My goal for these investigations is to find specific strategies that take you from big idea to big results—the type of strategies that can transform the missions in my notebooks from being merely ideas to becoming the foundation of an attention-catching career. We'll start with the story of a brash young archaeologist from a small town in Southeast Texas: someone who discovered a systematic strategy for deploying a bold mission in a field famous for its conformity.

American Treasures

I first encountered Kirk French while watching the Discovery Channel. During a commercial break, I saw an ad for the network's newest show. It was called *American Treasures*. The spot showed a pair of young archaeologists, dressed in jeans and battered work shirts, driving around the American backcountry in an old Ford F-150, helping people determine the historical significance of their family heirlooms. The hosts, who were revealed to be archaeologists Kirk French and Jason De León, seemed loud and energetic and enjoying the hell out of what they were doing. It was like *Antiques Roadshow*, but with considerably more drinking and cursing. I set my DVR to record the premiere.

Early in this first episode, Kirk and Jason find themselves in the East Texas flatlands, at a run-down, dirt-road homestead. They are there to investigate the authenticity of a suit of clothes that supposedly belonged to Clyde Barrow of Bonnie and Clyde fame.

It takes the archaeologists all of thirty seconds to disprove this claim: Not a lot of suits from that period feature a "Made in China" tag. But this doesn't dampen their enthusiasm.

"You're from a moonshine family," notes French.

"Yep," drawls Leslie, the suit's owner.

"Let's try some moonshine."

Soon a glass pitcher is produced. As Leslie pours the hootch into Mason jars, he offers a warning: "Don't ask about the proof. You wouldn't drink it if you knew." As Kirk and Jason sit on a pair of logs, drinking the moonshine and swapping stories, surrounded by East Texas nothingness, they seem to be having a great time.

I was hooked. To understand the appeal of *American Treasures*, you must understand its competition. At the time, cable TV was overrun with "cash for junk"–style shows, such as the History Channel's *Pawn Stars*, which follows the staff of a Las Vegas pawnshop as they try to bargain cash-strapped people out of valuable possessions; and the Discovery Channel's *Auction Kings*, which follows the adventures of an Atlanta-based auction house whose website deploys significantly more exclamation points than, say, Sotheby's might approve of. These shows, of course, are not to be confused with Discovery's *American Pickers*, which also follows a team that buys people's possessions, but now features the key twist that the bargain hunters travel in a van instead of working out of a storefront. And none of these should be confused with either Discovery's *Auction Hunters* or the History Channel's *Storage Wars*, both of which take a hard-hitting look at buying abandoned storage units at auction—a topic too nuanced, it seems, to be fully plumbed by only a single series.

These programs never interested me. But something about *American Treasures* caught my attention. I think once I looked past the name—which Kirk later admitted to me he both hated and fought against—I was struck by the fact that the hosts had a purpose beyond just wanting to be on television. For one thing, they aren't full-time TV personalities, but are instead academic archaeologists. (The Discovery Channel had to buy out a semester of their teaching obligations so they could film the first season.) In addition, there's no exchanging of cash in this show (a mainstay of all other entries in this genre). Putting monetary value on artifacts is antithetical to the mission of archaeology, and Kirk and Jason refused to do so in their show. The hosts instead seem driven by the idea that they're educating the public about the reality of modern archaeology. This is their mission, and as indicated by the smiles on their faces as they sipped East Texas moonshine in the premiere episode of their show, it's a mission that's a hell of a lot of fun to pursue.

Not long after meeting Pardis Sabeti, around the time I started questioning why I didn't have a mission-driven career, Kirk and Jason popped back to mind. I realized that they provided a perfect case study of what it's like to leap a large gap between idea and practice. The mission of popularizing archaeology to a mass audience, and having a fun time doing so, sounds good on paper, but to actually devote your career to this mission, especially when you're just out of graduate school and trying to make a name for yourself in a traditional academic field, is a terrifying prospect. I called up Kirk to find out what strategy he used to make this leap with confidence.

The Armchair Archaeologist

No one who knows him would describe Kirk French as boring. "After Bush won the election in 2004," he told me, "I sort of lost it. I sold everything and moved to the woods." The "woods" consisted of sixteen acres of old farmland, and it was a twenty-minute drive from the Penn State campus, where Kirk was a graduate student at the time.

While living in his "hermit" mode, he decided to build a wooden stage in an apple tree grove not far from his cabin and organize a music festival, which he called, naturally, Kirk Fest. Jason De León, a fellow grad student at Penn State, had a band named Wilcox Hotel at the time, which played at the festival. He admired Kirk's entrepreneurial streak and asked if he wanted to manage Wilcox Hotel. Kirk thought it sounded like fun. They ended up taking time off from their graduate studies to buy a minibus and "drive across the country and back" on tour. They also recorded two CDs during this period. I tell these stories because they emphasize that Kirk is someone who is not afraid to try something bold if it holds out the promise of making his life more interesting.

During this period as a graduate student, Kirk, who specialized in Mayan water management, was interviewed

for a History Channel documentary on the Maya called
Lost Worlds. As someone always seeking creative outlets for
his energy, this experience helped Kirk cement a potential
mission for his career: to popularize modern archaeology
to a mass audience. His first efforts to explore this direction began after he graduated with his PhD and became
a postdoc, and they centered on a classic 1961 documentary called *Land and Water: An Ecological Study of the Teotihuacan Valley of Mexico*, filmed by the late Penn State
archaeologist William Sanders. This film documents how
the rise of Mexico City has transformed the ecology and
lifestyle in the Teotihuacan Valley. For those, like Kirk,
who study historical ecology, it's an influential film.

In the fall of 2009, Kirk got his hands on the original 16 mm reels, including outtakes that never made the
original cut, as well as Sanders's notes. He launched two
projects surrounding this find. The first was to digitize
the original film footage and release a DVD of the original documentary—a project he completed in the spring
of 2010. The second project was more ambitious. He
decided to film a new version of the documentary—an
update that would show the further changes that have
happened between the 1960s and the present in the valley. Kirk raised seed money from Penn State's anthropology department and the Maya Exploration Center,
put together a team, and in the winter of 2010 headed
down to Mexico City to begin filming sample footage.
The goal was to pull together enough compelling shots

to "convince funding agencies of the importance of [the project]."

Kirk's breakthrough for his mission, however, began in December 2009. George Milner, a professor in the office next to Kirk, called him in to join a group of archaeologists who were all standing around Milner's phone. "You've got to listen to this message," he said while dialing in to his voice mail. The recording was of a man who lived just north of Pittsburgh. He sounded articulate and thoughtful—at least, until he got to the reason he was calling the Penn State archaeology department. "I've got what I think is the treasure of the Knights Templar in my backyard," he explained.

The gathered academics all had a good laugh. But then Kirk interjected: "I'm going to call him back." His more experienced colleagues tried to talk him out of it. "He will never leave you alone," they told him. "He will call you back every week and keep asking you questions."

As Kirk explained to me, in an academic field like archaeology, you get a lot of these types of calls—"people who think they found a dinosaur footprint, or whatever"—and there's just not time, with the pressure of research and teaching, to keep up with them. But Kirk saw an opportunity here that would support his mission. "This type of public outreach is exactly what we archaeologists *should* be doing," he realized.

He decided he was going to follow up on the random calls that came in to the department. He planned to go meet the people, hear their stories, and help explain how the principles of archaeology can lead them to figure out whether or not a medieval organization of knights was actually traipsing around the hills of Pittsburgh. Not only would he meet them but he would also film the encounters, with the eventual goal of producing a documentary on the most interesting case. He called the project *The Armchair Archaeologist.* He envisioned this side project taking five or ten years—something to work on alongside his filming in the Teotihuacan Valley. "I figured, at the very least, I could show it to the students in my intro archaeology classes," he said.

On a Sunday morning, not long after hearing the call about the Knights Templar treasure, Kirk gathered a cameraman and soundman, and headed out to Pittsburgh to investigate the claim. "He was the coolest guy," Kirk recalls. "He had crazy ideas, but he was fun to talk to. We hung out all day, and had some beers, and chatted." The "treasure," it turns out, was just some old deer bones and railroad spikes found in a gravel pit, but the experience was invigorating for Kirk. It also turned out to be more consequential than he could ever have guessed.

Around this time, the Discovery Channel decided it wanted a reality show that had something to do with archaeology. As is common in the TV business, instead of developing the idea themselves, the channel instead spread word of their general interest, and left it to independent production companies to pull together specific show concepts. Three months after Kirk filmed his Pittsburgh footage, one of these production companies contacted the head of the archaeology department at Penn State, who forwarded the message to the whole staff. "Sure I had only three months of experience on my job as a lecturer at the time," Kirk recalled, "but I was really interested in media, so I thought, 'Why not me?'" Kirk followed up with the production company. "I have your show idea," he told them, not long into their initial conversation. He sent them his *Armchair Archaeologist* footage.

The production company loved the idea and they loved Kirk. They refilmed his visit to the Templars' treasure site and sent the tape to the Discovery Channel and the History Channel. The latter agreed to finance a pilot, but the former said, "Screw a pilot, let's film eight episodes." When they asked Kirk about a cohost, he had only one name to offer, his good friend Jason De León, who had also recently graduated Penn State and had just started as an assistant professor at Michigan. They both arranged for the Discovery Channel to buy out their teaching obligations for the following fall, and then hit the road to film the first season of what would become *American Treasures*.[1]

Leveraging Little Bets

Kirk's mission was to popularize archaeology, and he wanted to do so in a way that generated an exciting life.

Hosting *American Treasures* made this mission a reality. The question at hand is how he made this leap from a general idea into specific action.

Here's what I noticed: Kirk's path to *American Treasures* was incremental. He didn't decide out of nowhere that he wanted to host a television show and then work backward to make that dream a reality. Instead, he worked forward from his original mission—to popularize archaeology—with a series of small, almost tentative steps. When he stumbled on the old film reels for *Land and Water*, for example, he decided to digitize them and produce a DVD. After this small step he took the slightly larger step of raising money to shoot exploratory footage for a new version of the documentary. When George Milner played him that fateful answering machine tape, Kirk took another modest step by launching *The Armchair Archaeologist* project with no real vision of how it would prove useful, other than perhaps as fodder for his intro archaeology courses. This final little step, however, turned out to be a winner, leading directly to his own television show.

As I was struggling to make sense of Kirk's story, I stumbled across a new business book that had been making waves. It was titled *Little Bets*, and it was written by a former venture capitalist named Peter Sims.[2] When Sims studied a variety of successful innovators, from Steve Jobs to Chris Rock to Frank Gehry, as well as innovative companies, such as Amazon and Pixar, he found a strategy common to all. "Rather than believing they have to start with a big idea or plan out a whole project in advance," he writes, "they make a methodical series of *little bets* about what might be a good direction, learning critical information from lots of little failures and from small but significant wins" [emphasis mine]. This rapid and frequent feedback, Sims argues, "allows them to find unexpected avenues and arrive at extraordinary outcomes."

To illustrate this idea, Sims details the example of Chris Rock preparing a comedy set for one of his acclaimed HBO specials. Rock, it turns out, will make somewhere between forty to fifty unannounced visits to a small New Jersey–area comedy club to help him figure out which material works and which doesn't. As Sims notes, he shows up on stage with a yellow legal pad, working through different jokes, taking notes on the crowd's reaction. Most of the material falls flat. It's not uncommon for Rock to look up and say, "This needs to be fleshed out more," while the crowd laughs at the awkwardness of Rock's flops. But these little failures, combined with the little victories of the jokes that connect, provide the key information required for Rock to put together an extraordinary set.

This style of little bets, I realized, is what Kirk deployed to feel out his mission of popularizing archaeology. He tried releasing a DVD, filming a documentary, and putting together a film series for his students. The latter ended up the most promising, but Kirk couldn't have known this in advance. The important thing about little bets is that they're bite-sized. You try one. It takes a few months at most. It either succeeds or fails, but either way you get important feedback to guide your next steps. This approach stands in contrast to the idea of choosing a bold plan and making one big bet on its success. If Kirk had done this—for example, deciding in advance to dedicate years to popularizing the *Land and Water* documentary—he would not have had nearly as much success with his mission.

When I looked back to Pardis Sabeti's story, I noticed the little-bets strategy at play here as well. As you'll recall, she decided early in her graduate student career to pursue the general mission of tackling infectious disease in Africa. But at this stage, she didn't know how to make this mission successful, so she launched small experiments. She started in a research lab working on the genetic heritage of African-Americans. This didn't seem quite right, so she moved to a group that worked on malaria—but again, she didn't see a clear path to making her mission a success. Returning to Harvard, she began work as a postdoctoral fellow at the Broad Institute. It was here that she began to gain traction for her computational approach to seeking out markers of natural selection in the human genome. It was this last bet—out of a long string of such bets—that proved to be a big winner, at which point she dedicated her career to its pursuit. It was tentativeness, not boldness, that transformed Pardis's general mission into a specific success.

A Brief Mission Intermission

Let's take a moment to pull together what we've learned so far about mission. In the last chapter, I used Pardis Sabeti's story to emphasize that you need career capital before you can identify a realistic mission for your career. Just because you have a good idea for a mission, however, doesn't mean that you'll succeed in its pursuit. With this in mind, in this chapter we studied the life of Kirk French to better understand how you make the leap from identifying a realistic mission to succeeding in making it a reality.

Here we discovered the importance of little bets. To maximize your chances of success, you should deploy small, concrete experiments that return concrete feedback. For Chris Rock, such a bet might include telling a joke to an audience and seeing if they laugh, whereas for Kirk, it might mean producing sample footage for a documentary and seeing if it attracts funding. These bets allow you to tentatively explore the specific avenues surrounding your general mission, looking for those with the highest likelihood of leading to outstanding results.

If career capital makes it possible to identify a compelling mission, then it's a strategy of little bets that gives you a good shot of succeeding in this mission. To deploy this career tactic, you need both pieces. As you'll learn in the next chapter, however, the story of mission is not yet complete. As I continued my study of this topic, I discovered a third and final strategy for helping to integrate this trait into your quest for work you love.

Chapter Fifteen

Missions Require Marketing

*In which I argue that great missions are transformed into great successes as the result of finding projects that satisfy the **law of remarkability**, which requires that an idea inspires people to remark about it, and is launched in a venue where such remarking is made easy.*

The Remarkable Life of Giles Bowkett

Giles Bowkett loves what he does for a living. In fact, my first encounter with Giles was an e-mail he sent me with the subject line: "My remarkable life."

Giles, however, didn't always love his career. There were points when he was broke and unemployed, and other points when he suffered through jobs that bored him into a stupor. The turning point came in 2008 when Giles became a rock star in the community of computer programmers who specialize in a language called Ruby. "It seems as if every Ruby programmer on the planet knows my name," he told me, reflecting on his newfound celebrity. "I literally met people from Argentina and Norway who not only knew who I was but were absolutely shocked that I didn't *expect* them to know who I was."

I'll dive into the details of *how* Giles became a star soon, but what I want to emphasize now is that this fame allowed him to take control of his career and to transform it into something he loves. "I had a lot of interest from companies in San Francisco and Silicon Valley," he told me, reflecting on the period that began in 2008. He decided to take a job with ENTP, one of the country's top Ruby programming firms. They doubled his salary and put him to work on interesting projects. In 2009, Giles was bit by an entrepreneurial bug. He left ENTP and built up a blog and a collection of mini–Web applications that soon brought in enough money to support him. "I had an audience who wanted to know what I thought about a whole ton of different things," he told me. "In many cases they were happy to pay money just to ask me questions."

Eventually, he decided that he had had his fill with the solo lifestyle ("working from home is kind of lame when you don't have roommates, a girlfriend, or even a dog"), so he pursued a longstanding interest in filmmaking by going to work for hitRECord: a company started by actor Joseph Gordon-Levitt that provides a Web-based platform for collaborative media projects. It's not that the money was great ("the Hollywood understanding of what programmers get paid is wildly inaccurate"), but just that it sounded like a lot of fun—one of Giles's most important criteria for his working life. "It was a pretty great experience," he told me. "I got to hang out with one of the stars of *Inception* and the next *Batman*, drinking beers at his house, that kind of thing." Not long after I met Giles, after he had successfully scratched his Hollywood itch, he once again moved on. A publisher had asked him to write a book, and he had agreed—and why not? It seemed like an interesting thing to do.

The speed with which Giles bounces from opportunity to opportunity might seem disorienting, but this lifestyle is a perfect match for his hyperkinetic personality. One of Giles's favorite presentation techniques, for example, is to begin talking faster and faster, accompanying his speech with a rapid series of slides, each featuring a single keyword that flashes on the screen at the exact moment that he utters the term—the oratorical equivalent of a caffeine rush. In other words, he used his capital to build a career custom-fit to his personality, which is why he now loves his working life.

The reason I'm telling Giles's story here in Rule #4 is that at the core of his rise to fame was his *mission*. In more detail, Giles committed himself to the mission of bringing together the worlds of art and Ruby programming. He made good on this commitment when he released Archaeopteryx, an open-source artificial intelligence program that writes and plays its own dance music. Watching Archaeopteryx in action can be eerie: An innocuous command typed into the Mac command line starts an aggressive and complicated techno break-beat; a single value is changed in the Bayesian probability matrices underlying the AI engine; and all of a sudden the beat transforms into something entirely different. It's as if musical creativity itself has been reduced to a series of equations and some lines of terse code. This feat made Giles a star.

But the question that interests me most about Giles is how he made the leap from a general mission—to bring together art and Ruby programming—to a specific, fame-inducing project: Archaeopteryx. In the last chapter, I highlighted the importance of using *little bets* to feel out a good way forward from general mission to specific project. Giles, however, adds another layer of nuance to this goal. He approached the task of finding good projects for his mission with the mindset of a marketer, systematically studying books on the subject to help identify why some ideas catch on while others fall flat. His marketing-centric approach is useful for anyone looking to wield mission as part of their quest for work they love.

Purple Cows and Open-Source Rock Stars

Giles's career story starts when he left Santa Fe College after his first year. He tried writing screenplays, "but they weren't good," and he tried writing music, "which I was better at, but which didn't pay." He also temped. Artistic in nature, Giles was drawn to the graphic designers in the companies where he worked and they introduced him to quirky new markup language that was poised to change the world of design—a language called HTML. Giles built his first Web page in 1994, and in 1996 he moved to San Francisco, bringing with him books on Java and Perl, programming languages that provided the foundation of the early Web. He made $30,000 in 1994. In 1996 this jumped to $100,000: The dot-com boom was picking up speed and Giles was in the right place with the right skills at the right time.

At first, things went well for Giles in San Francisco. He enjoyed designing websites and in his free time he became involved in the local DJ scene. But careers have their own sort of momentum, and he soon found himself programming for an investment bank. "I was bored out of my mind," he recalls, "so I decided to do something bold: I was going to apply to a really interesting start-up." The day after he submitted his application the start-up went under. The first dot-com crash had begun. "Pretty soon I was the only one of my friends who had a job at all," he recalled. "I talked to a recruiter about finding something I liked better, and he said I should be thrilled to have a job."

Giles being Giles, however, he ignored the recruiter, quit his job, and moved back to Santa Fe. He lived in a rented camper on his parents' land, helping them build a solar-powered house while taking courses at the local community college. He studied painting, voice, piano, and perhaps most importantly, studio engineering, the class that introduced him to aleatoric music: composition using algorithms. It's here, among the desert landscapes and arts courses, that Giles made a key decision. A career untamed, he realized, can bring you into dangerous territory, such as being bored while writing computer code for an investment bank. He needed a *mission* to actively guide his career or he would end up trapped again and again. He decided that a good mission for him would somehow combine the artistic and technical sides of his life, but he didn't know how to make this general idea into a money-making reality, so he went searching for answers. He found what he was looking for in an unlikely pair of books.

———

"You're either remarkable or invisible," says Seth Godin in his 2002 bestseller, *Purple Cow.*[1] As he elaborated in a *Fast Company* manifesto he published on the subject: "The world is full of boring stuff—brown cows—which is why so few people pay attention....A purple cow... now that would stand out. Remarkable marketing is the art of building things worth noticing."[2] When Giles read Godin's book, he had an epiphany: For his mission to build a sustainable career, it had to produce purple cows, the type of remarkable projects that compel people to spread the word.

But this left him with a second question: In the world

of computer programming, where does one launch remarkable projects? He found his second answer in a 2005 career guide with a quirky title: *My Job Went to India: 52 Ways to Save Your Job.*[3] The book was written by Chad Fowler, a well-known Ruby programmer who also dabbles in career advice for software developers. Featured among Fowler's fifty-two strategies is the idea that the job seeker should leverage the open-source software movement. This movement brings together computer programmers who volunteer their time to build software that's freely available and modifiable. Fowler argued that this community is well respected and highly visible. If you want to make a name for yourself in software development—the type of name that can help you secure employment—focus your attention on making quality contributions to open-source projects. This is where the people who matter look for talent.

"At this point I basically just put two and two together," Giles told me. "The synthesis of *Purple Cow* and *My Job Went to India* is that the best way to market yourself as a programmer is to create remarkable open-source software. So I did."

Following Godin's advice, Giles came up with the idea for Archaeopteryx, his AI-driven music creator. "I don't think there was anybody else with my combined background," he said. "Plenty of Ruby programmers love dance music, but I don't think any of them has sacrificed the same ridiculous number of hours to tweaking breakbeats and synth patches over and over again, releasing white-label records that never made a dime, and studying music theory." In other words, Giles's ability to produce a Ruby program that produced real music was unique: If he could pull it off, it would be a purple cow.

Drawing from Fowler's advice, Giles then decided that the open-source community was the perfect place to introduce this purple cow to the world. In addition to releasing the Archaeopteryx code as open source, he took to the road to spread the word. "I basically took Chad Fowler's advice *way* too far and went to speak at almost every user group and conference that I could—at least fifteen in 2008," Giles recalled. This hybrid Godin/Fowler strategy worked. "I got offers from all over the place," Giles recalled. "I got to work with stars in my industry, I got approached to write a book on Archaeopteryx, I could charge a lot more money than I used to." It was, in other words, a strategy that made his mission into a success.

The Law of Remarkability

Reflecting on Giles's story, I kept coming back to the same adjective: "remarkable." What Giles discovered, I decided, is that a good mission-driven project must be remarkable in two different ways. First, it should be remarkable in the literal sense of compelling people to remark about it. To understand this trait, let's first look at something that *lacks* it. Before releasing Archaeopteryx, Giles had worked on another open-source project. He collected popular command-line tools for Ruby and combined them into one package with consistent documentation. If you asked a Ruby programmer about this project, he would tell you that this is solid, quality, useful work. But it's not the type of achievement that would compel this same Ruby programmer to write his friends and tell them, "You *have* to see this!"

In the words of Seth Godin, this early project was a "brown cow." By contrast, teaching your computer to write its own complex music is a purple cow; it inspires people to take notice and spread the word.

What's nice about this first notion of remarkability is that it can be applied to any field. Take book writing: If I published a book of solid advice for helping recent graduates transition to the job market, you might find this a useful contribution, but probably wouldn't find yourself whipping out your iPhone and Tweeting its praises. On the other hand, if I publish a book that says "follow your passion" is bad advice, (hopefully) this would compel you to spread the word. That is, the book you're holding was conceived from the very early stages with the hope of being seen as "remarkable."

There's also, however, a second type of remarkability at play. Giles didn't just find a project that compels remarks, but he also spread the word about the project in a venue that *supports* these remarks. In his case, this venue was the open-source software community. As he learned from Chad Fowler, there's an established infrastructure in this community for noticing and spreading the word about interesting projects. Without this conduciveness to chatter, a purple cow, though striking, may never be seen. To be more concrete, if Giles had instead released Archaeopteryx as a closed-source piece of commercial software, perhaps trying to sell it from a slick website or at music conventions, it probably wouldn't have caught fire as it did.

Once again, this notion of remarkability applies beyond just Giles's world of Ruby programming. If we return to my example of writing career-advice books, I realized early on in my process that blogging was a remarkable venue for introducing my ideas. Blogs are visible and the infrastructure is in place for good ideas to quickly spread, through, for example, linking, Tweets, and Facebook. Because of this conduciveness to remarking, by the time I pitched this book to publishers, I not only had a large audience who appreciated my views on passion and skill, but the meme had spread: Newspapers and major websites around the world had begun to quote my thoughts on the topic, while the articles had been cited online and Tweeted thousands of times. If I had instead decided to confine my ideas to paid speaking gigs, for example, my mission to change the way we think about careers would have likely stagnated—the venue would not have been sufficiently remarkable.

To help organize our thinking, I'll summarize these ideas in a succinct law:

The Law of Remarkability

*For a mission-driven project to succeed, it should be **remarkable** in two different ways. First, it must compel people who encounter it to remark about it to others. Second, it must be launched in a venue that supports such remarking.*

Once I had articulated this law, I began to notice it at play in the examples I had previously found of mission leading to a compelling career. To help cement this marketing-centric approach to mission, it's worth taking a moment to return to these examples and highlight the law in action.

The Law in Action

Pardis Sabeti's general mission was to use genetics to help fight infectious disease in Africa. This is a fine mission, but by itself it does not guarantee the type of fulfilling life Pardis leads. In fact, lots of researchers share this mission, and are doing good, basic science—such as sequencing the genes of viruses—but don't have particularly compelling careers. Pardis, by contrast, pursued this mission by launching an arresting project: using powerful computers to seek out examples of humans evolving resistance to ancient diseases. If you want evidence of the remarkability of this approach, look no farther than the catchy headlines of the many articles that have been penned on the Sabeti Lab—articles with titles such as "5 Questions for the Woman Who Tracks Our DNA Footprints" (*Discover*, April 2010), "Picking Up Evolution's Beat" (*Science*, April 2008), and "Are We Still Evolving?" (*BBC Horizon*, March 2011). This is a project that compels people to spread the word. It is a purple cow.

By seeking a remarkable project, Pardis satisfied the first part of the law of remarkability. The second part requires that she launch her project in a venue that supports remarking. For Pardis, as with all scientists, this is the easy part. Peer-reviewed publication is a system built around the idea of allowing good ideas to spread. The better the idea, the better the journal it gets published in. The better the journal an article is published in, the more people who read it. And the more people who read it, the more it gets cited, discussed at conferences, and in general affects the field. If you're a scientist with a remarkable idea, there's little doubt about how best to spread it: publish! This is exactly what Pardis did with the *Nature* article that jump-started her reputation.

With Kirk French, we also see the law of remarkability in action. His general mission was to popularize modern archaeology. There are lots of non-remarkable ways to pursue this mission. For example, he could have worked on making the archaeology curriculum at Penn

State more appealing to undergraduates, or published articles on the field in general-interest science magazines. But these projects would not have generated the type of attention-grabbing success that can transform your career into something compelling. Instead, Kirk decided to head straight into people's homes and use archaeological techniques to help them uncover the significance (if any) of family treasures. This approach *is* remarkable—an observation reinforced by the number of speaking invitations Kirk now receives, including a recent opportunity to address the largest conference in his field about lessons learned as a popularizer. When he gave the address, the crowd overflowed the auditorium (an impressive feat for someone who had just earned his doctorate).

In this example, Kirk had a remarkable project to support his mission—now all he needed was a venue conducive to remarking. He found this remarkable venue with television. We're a society trained to watch what's on and then discuss what caught our attention the next day.

Summary of Rule #4

The core idea of this book is simple: To construct work you love, you must first build career capital by mastering rare and valuable skills, and then cash in this capital for the type of traits that define compelling careers. **Mission** is one of those traits.

In the first chapter of this rule, I reinforced the idea that this trait, like all desirable career traits, really does require career capital—you can't skip straight into a great mission without first building mastery in your field. Drawing from the terminology of Steven Johnson, I argued that the best ideas for missions are found in the **adjacent possible**—the region just beyond the current cutting edge.

To encounter these ideas, therefore, you must first get to that cutting edge, which in turn requires expertise. To try to devise a mission when you're new to a field and lacking any career capital is a venture bound for failure.

Once you identify a general mission, however, you're still left with the task of launching specific projects that make it succeed. An effective strategy for accomplishing this task is to try small steps that generate concrete feedback—**little bets**—and then use this feedback, be it good or bad, to help figure out what to try next. This systematic exploration can help you uncover an exceptional way forward that you might have never otherwise noticed.

The little-bets strategy, I discovered as my research into mission continued, is not the only way to make a mission a success. It also helps to adopt the mindset of a marketer. This led to the strategy that I dubbed the **law of remarkability**.

This law says that for a project to transform a mission into a success, it should be remarkable in two ways. First, it must literally compel people to remark about it. Second, it must be launched in a venue conducive to such remarking.

In sum, mission is one of the most important traits you can acquire with your career capital. But adding this trait to your working life is not simple. Once you have the capital to identify a good mission, you must still work to make it succeed. By using little bets and the law of remarkability, you greatly increase your chances of finding ways to transform your mission from a compelling idea into a compelling career.

Conclusion

My Story Resumes

In the introduction to this book I described the circumstances that launched me on the quest you just finished reading about. My time as a graduate student and postdoc was winding down, and I was about to enter the academic-job market. Succeeding as a professor, I knew, was not an easy task. If you're not in control of your career, it can chew you up and spit you out. To make matters worse, I was entering the market in a bad economy, so there was a chance I might not find a suitable academic position at all, which would force me to start from scratch in my career thinking. This uncertainty made the following question suddenly seem pressing: *How do people end up loving what they do?*

In the fall of 2010 I sent out my applications for academic jobs. By early December I had applied to twenty positions. A curious quirk of the academic-job search process is that your colleagues expect it to be demanding, so they keep tasks off your desk. And though the process is in fact demanding, these demands come in bursts, leaving long stretches of downtime in between. Without much work to fill these stretches, you can find yourself uncomfortably idle. So it was that as November gave way to December, and I finished submitting my twenty applications, I had, for the first time since my college summer vacations, not much to do.

With free time on my hands, I could finally begin to tackle my quest in earnest. It was at this point that I began to seek out people's career stories, both successes and failures, to see what I could learn. It was in November, for example, that I first met Thomas, whose tale opened this book. The stories I encountered that fall cemented an idea that I had long suspected to be true: "Follow your passion" is bad advice. But this validation only brought forward the more difficult task of figuring out what career-happiness strategies *do* work.

My search for this answer was put on hold in January and February as my job search process picked up steam. I began to prepare my job talk and sift through the interview offers that started to trickle in. In early March I went on an interview trip that included a stop at Georgetown University. Everything about Georgetown felt right. Fortunately, I had another offer at the time with a tight deadline. I told my contacts at Georgetown that I enjoyed my visit and was interested in the position but that I had a fast-approaching deadline. Later that night

I received the key e-mail from the head of their search committee. It was terse, just three sentences:

> *We will have an offer for you on Thursday. We just need to know where to contact you to communicate it in the afternoon. Will your cell phone be the best way to reach you?* ·

I turned down a pair of interviews that had been scheduled for later in the spring and accepted the Georgetown offer. My career die had been cast: I was going to be a professor. It was the second week of March when I formally took myself off the market. My start date would be in August. This left a gap of four months to finalize my answers to my pressing career questions: I now had a job, but I needed to figure out how to transform it into one I loved. During that spring and subsequent summer, I hit the road, conducting the interviews that formed the core of Rules #2–4.

As I'm writing this conclusion, I'm now two weeks away from my first semester as a professor. I have been working hard over the past several months to not only finish the quest I described in this book, but also to write up my experiences in the form in which you just encountered them. (I signed the deal for this book only two weeks after accepting my Georgetown offer.) This conclusion is the last piece of this book to be written, and the timing couldn't be better. I'll be handing in this manuscript mere days before turning my attention to my new life as a professor—allowing me to start this new chapter of my career with confidence in what I should do to push it somewhere remarkable.

My quest, of course, uncovered several surprising ideas. If your goal is to love what you do, I discovered, "follow you passion" can be bad advice. It's more important to become good at something rare and valuable, and then invest the *career capital* this generates into the type of traits that make a job great. The traits of *control* and *mission* are two good places to start. My goal for this final part of the book is to describe how I am applying these ideas in my own working life. That is, I want to take you inside my thought process and highlight the specific ways in which the insights of Rules #1–4 are playing a role in this early stage of my new career. Obviously these applications are tentative—I have not yet been a professor long enough to see how they will all play out—but it's this tentativeness, I think, that makes them more relevant. They provide a real-world example of the type of concrete actions you can take *right now* to start applying the lessons of this book in your own working life. Your decisions will differ from mine, but I hope that you'll encounter in this conclusion a better sense of what it means to re-form a career to match this new way of thinking about creating work you love.

How I Applied Rule #1

Rule #1 argued that "follow your passion" is bad advice, as the vast majority of people don't have pre-existing passions waiting to be discovered and matched to a career. The real path to work you love, it noted, is often more complicated. This insight was not one that I encountered for the first time during my quest, but was instead something I had long suspected to be true. Although the chapter on Rule #1 describes my recent efforts to find real evidence for this intuition, the seeds for this thought had been planted long before.

The story of my passion aversion starts in high school, when my friend Michael Simmons and I started a Web design company. We called it Princeton Web Solutions. The origin of our company was modest. It was the late 1990s—the first dot-com boom—and the media was obsessed with stories of teenage CEOs earning millions. Michael and I thought this sounded like fun—certainly a better way to make money than our standard summer jobs. We tried to think up a creative new idea for a high-tech company—something along the lines of a new Amazon.com—but we were stumped and ended up defaulting to an idea that we had earlier vowed we wouldn't pursue: designing websites. To be clear, we were by no means following our true calling. We were bored, available, and ambitious—a dangerous combination—and starting a company sounded as promising as anything else we could imagine.

Princeton Web Solutions wasn't a meteoric success, but this was partly by design, as we didn't really want to invest the time required to grow a serious company. During our senior year of high school we worked with six or seven clients, including a local architecture firm, a local technical college, and an ill-conceived—but oddly well-funded—Web portal targeting the elderly. Most of these contracts paid between $5,000 and $10,000, a healthy chunk of which we passed on to a team of Indian subcontractors, who did most of the actual programming work. When Michael and I left for college—he to NYU and I to Dartmouth—I decided I was done with website design and moved on to more pressing interests, such as girls.

For many in my generation, the rejection of "follow your passion" as career advice is heretical. I never felt this same attraction to the cult of passion, and for this I give credit to my experience with Princeton Web Solutions. As I mentioned, starting this company had nothing to do with me following a passion. Once Michael and I figured out how to keep the business humming, however, this skill turned out to be rare and valuable (especially for people our age). This career capital could then be cashed in for a variety of different exciting experiences. We got to wear suits and make pitches to boardrooms. We made enough money to never have to worry about not being able to afford the types of things teenagers buy. Our teachers were impressed by the company and allowed us to unofficially ditch classes for meetings. Magazines wrote about us, photographers came to take our pictures for newspapers, and the whole experience certainly played a large role in our being admitted to elite colleges.

The traits that can make your life interesting, I learned, had very little to do with intensive soul-searching. Princeton Web Solutions, in other words, had inoculated me against the idea that occupational happiness requires a calling.

Because of these early experiences, I looked on with curiosity, once I arrived at college, when my classmates began to wring their hands about the question of what they wanted to do with their lives. For them, something as basic as choosing a major became weighted with cosmic significance. I thought this was nonsense. To me, the world was filled with opportunities like Princeton Web Solutions waiting to be exploited to make your life more interesting—opportunities that had nothing to do with identifying predestined dispositions.

Driven by this insight, while my classmates contemplated their true calling, I went seeking opportunities to master rare skills that would yield big rewards. I started by hacking my study skills to become as efficient as possible. This took one semester of systematic experiments and subsequently earned me three consecutive years of a 4.0 grade point average, a period during which I

never pulled an all-nighter and rarely studied past dinner. I then cashed in this asset by publishing a student-
advice guide. These experiences helped me build an
exciting student life—I was, I imagine, the only student
on Dartmouth's campus taking regular calls from his
literary agent—but neither came from the pursuit of a
pre-existing passion. Indeed, the motivation to write my
first book was an idle dare leveled by an entrepreneur I
admired whom I met one night for drinks: "Don't just talk
about it," he scolded me when I offhandedly mentioned
the book idea. "If you think it would be cool, go do it."
This seemed as good a reason as any for me to proceed.

When it later came time for me to decide what to do
after college, I had two offers in hand, one from Microsoft and the other from MIT. This is the type of decision
that would paralyze my classmates. I, however, didn't see
any reason to worry. Both paths, I was sure, would yield
numerous opportunities that could be leveraged into a
remarkable life. I ended up choosing MIT—among other
reasons, in order to stay closer to my girlfriend.

The point I'm trying to make in this section is that
the core insight of Rule #1 came to me *before* my quest
started, and in fact was something I internalized as early
as high school. When I came to the fall of 2011, therefore, and was facing the period of uncertainty when I
wasn't sure if I would become a professor or end up
doing something completely different, this Rule #1 mindset saved me from needless fretting about which of these

paths forward was my true calling. If tackled correctly, I was absolutely confident that either could yield a career I love. Figuring out how to achieve this goal, however, was less certain, and it was this question that led me to the insights described in Rules #2–4.

How I Applied Rule #2

Rule #1 argued that "follow your passion" is bad advice. This provided the motivation for my quest to figure out what *does* matter in creating work you love. Rule #2 described the first insight I encountered once my quest was under way. The things that make great work great, it argued, are rare and valuable. If you want them in your career, you need rare and valuable skills to offer in return. In other words, if you're not putting in the effort to become, as Steve Martin put it, "so good they can't ignore you," you're not likely to end up loving your work—regardless of whether or not you believe it's your true calling.

I introduced the term *career capital* to describe these rare and valuable skills, and noted that the tricky part is figuring out how to acquire this capital. By definition, if it's rare and valuable, it's not easy to get. This insight brought me into the world of performance science, where I encountered the concept of *deliberate practice*—a method for building skills by ruthlessly stretching yourself beyond where you're comfortable.

As I discovered, musicians, athletes, and chess players, among others, know all about deliberate practice, but knowledge workers do not. Most knowledge workers avoid the uncomfortable strain of deliberate practice like the plague, a reality emphasized by the typical cubicle dweller's obsessive e-mail–checking habit—for what is this behavior if not an escape from work that's more mentally demanding?

As I researched these ideas, I became increasingly worried about the current state of my academic career. I feared that my rate of acquiring career capital was tapering off. To understand this worry, you should understand that graduate school, and the postdoctoral years that often follow, provide an uneven growth experience. Early in this process you're constantly pushed into intellectual discomfort. A graduate-level mathematics problem set—something I have plenty of experience with—is about as pure an exercise in deliberate practice as you're likely to find. You're given a problem that you have no idea how to solve, but you *have* to solve it or you'll get a bad grade, so you dive in and try as hard as you can, repeatedly failing as different avenues lead you to dead ends. The mental strain of mustering every last available neuron toward solving a problem, driven by the fear of earning zero points on the assignment, is a nice encapsulation of exactly what the deliberate-practice literature says is necessary to improve. This is why, early in their careers, graduate students experience great leaps in their abilities.[1]

But at a research-oriented program like the one offered by MIT's computer science department, your course work winds down after the first two years. Soon after, your research efforts are expected to release themselves from your advisor's orbit and follow a self-directed trajectory. It's here that if you're not careful to keep pushing forward, your improvement can taper off to what the performance scientist Anders Ericsson called an "acceptable level," where you then remain stuck. The research driving Rule #2 taught me that these plateaus are dangerous because they cut off your supply of career capital and therefore cripple your ability to keep actively shaping your working life. As my quest continued, therefore, it became clear that I needed to introduce some practical strategies into my own working life that would force me to once again make deliberate practice a regular companion in my daily routine.

According to popular legend, Richard Feynman, the Nobel Prize–winning theoretical physicist, scored only a slightly above-average IQ of 125 when he was tested in high school. In his memoirs, however, we find hints of how he rose from modest intelligence to genius, when he talks about his compulsion to tear down important papers and mathematical concepts until he could understand the concepts from the bottom up. It's possible, in other words, that his amazing intellect was less about a gift from God and more about a dedication to deliberate practice. Motivated by my research and examples such as Feynman, I decided that focusing my attention on a bottom-up understanding of my own field's most difficult results would be a good first step toward revitalizing my career capital stores.

To initiate these efforts, I chose a paper that was well cited in my research niche, but that was also considered obtuse and hard to follow. The paper focused on only a single result—the analysis of an algorithm that offers the best-known solution to a well-known problem. Many people have cited this result, but few have understood the details that support it. I decided that mastering this notorious paper would prove a perfect introduction to my new regime of self-enforced deliberate practice.

Here was my first lesson: This type of skill development is hard. When I got to the first tricky gap in the paper's main proof argument, I faced immediate internal resistance. It was as if my mind realized the effort I was about to ask it to expend, and in response it unleashed a wave of neuronal protest, distant at first, but then as I persisted increasingly tremendous, crashing over my concentration with mounting intensity.

To combat this resistance, I deployed two types of structure. The first type was *time structure*: "I am going to work on this for one hour," I would tell myself. "I don't care if I faint from the effort, or make no progress, for the next hour this is my whole world." But of course I wouldn't faint and eventually I would make progress.

It took, on average, ten minutes for the waves of resistance to die down. Those ten minutes were always difficult, but knowing that my efforts had a time limit helped ensure that the difficulty was manageable.

The second type of structure I deployed was *information structure*—a way of capturing the results of my hard focus in a useful form. I started by building a proof map that captured the dependencies between the different pieces of the proof. This was hard, but not too hard, and it got me warmed up in my efforts to understand the result. I then advanced from the maps to short self-administered quizzes that forced me to memorize the key definitions the proof used. Again, this was a relatively easy task, but it still took concentration, and the result was an understanding that was crucial for parsing the detailed math that came next.

After these first two steps, emboldened by my initial successes in deploying hard focus, I moved on to the big guns: proof summaries. This is where I forced myself to take each lemma and walk through each step of its proofs—filling in missing steps. I would conclude by writing a detailed summary in my own words. This was staggeringly demanding, but the fact that I had already spent time on easier tasks in the paper built up enough momentum to help push me forward.

I returned to this paper regularly over a period of two weeks. When I was done, I had probably experienced fifteen hours total of deliberate practice–style strain, but due to its intensity it felt like much more. Fortunately, this effort led to immediate benefits. Among other things, it allowed me to understand whole swaths of related work that had previously been mysterious. The researchers who wrote this paper had enjoyed a near monopoly on solving this style of problem—now I could join them. Leveraging this new understanding, I went on to prove a new result, which I published at a top conference in my field. This is now a new research direction open for me to explore as I see fit. Perhaps even more indicative of this strategy's value is that I actually ended up finding a pair of mistakes in the paper. When I told the authors, it turned out I was only the second person to notice them, and they hadn't yet published a correction. To help calibrate the magnitude of this omission, bear in mind that according to Google Scholar the paper had already been cited close to sixty times.

More important than these small successes, however, was the new mindset this test case introduced. Strain, I now accepted, was good. Instead of seeing this discomfort as a sensation to avoid, I began to understand it the same way that a body builder understands muscle burn: a sign that you're doing something right. Inspired by this insight, I accompanied a promise to do more large-scale paper deconstructions of this type with a trio of smaller habits designed to inject even more deliberate practice into my daily routine. I describe these new routines below:

My Research Bible Routine

At some point during my quest, I started what I came to call my *research bible,* which is, in reality, a document I keep on my computer. Here's the routine: Once a week I require myself to summarize in my "bible" a paper I think might be relevant to my research. This summary must include a description of the result, how it compares to previous work, and the main strategies used to obtain it. These summaries are less involved than the step-by-step deconstruction I did on my original test-case paper—which is what allows me to do them on a weekly basis—but they still induce the strain of deliberate practice.

My Hour-Tally Routine

Another deliberate-practice routine was the introduction of my *hour tally*—a sheet of paper I mounted behind my desk at MIT, and plan on remounting at Georgetown. The sheet has a row for each month on which I keep a tally of the total number of hours I've spent that month in a state of deliberate practice. I started the tally sheet on March 15, 2011, and in the last two weeks of that month I experienced 12 hours of strain. In April, the first full month of this record keeping, I got the tally up to 42 hours. In May, I backslid to 26.5 hours and in June this fell to 23 hours. (In fairness, these last two months were a period during which I was up to my ears in the logistics of switching from my position at MIT to my position at Georgetown.) By having these hour counts stare me in the face every day I'm motivated to find new ways to fit more deliberate practice into my schedule. Without this routine, my total amount of time spent stretching my abilities would undoubtedly be much lower.

My Theory-Notebook Routine

My third strategy was the purchase of the most expensive notebook I could find at the MIT bookstore: an archival-quality lab notebook that cost me forty-five dollars. This notebook boasts a nice thick cardboard cover, mounted on double-wire spirals, that falls open flat. The pages are acid-free, thick, and gridded. I use this notebook when brainstorming new theory results. At the end of each of these brainstorming sessions I require myself to formally record the results, by hand, on a dated page. The expense of the notebook helps signal the importance of what I'm supposed to write inside it, and this, in turn, forces me into the strain required to collect and organize my thinking. The result: more deliberate practice.

The insights of Rule #2 fundamentally changed the way I approach my work. If I had to describe my previous way of thinking, I would probably use the phrase "productivity-centric." Getting things done was my priority. When you adopt a productivity mindset, however, deliberate practice-inducing tasks are often sidestepped, as the ambiguous path toward their completion, when combined with the discomfort of the mental strain they require, makes them an unpopular choice in scheduling decisions. It's much easier to redesign your graduate-student Web page than it is to grapple with a mind-melting proof. The result for me was that my career capital stores, initially built up during the forced strain of my early years as a graduate student, were dwindling as time went on. Researching Rule #2, however, changed this state of affairs by making me much more "craft-centric." Getting better and better at what I did became what mattered most, and getting better required the strain of deliberate practice. This is a different way of thinking about work, but once you embrace it, the changes to your career trajectory can be profound.

How I Applied Rule #3

In the early spring of 2011, my academic-job hunt took an interesting turn. At the time, I had a verbal offer from Georgetown University, but nothing in writing, and as my postdoctoral advisor told me, "If it's not in writing, it doesn't count." While waiting for the official offer, I received an interview invitation from a well-known state university with a well-funded research program. Deciding how to navigate this career conundrum was vastly simplified by my quest, which was under way at the same time. In particular, it was my investigation of the value of *control*, as detailed in Rule #3, that provided me guidance.

Rule #3 argued that control over what you do and how you do it is such a powerful force for building remarkable careers that it could rightly be called a "dream-job elixir." When you study the type of careers that make others remark, *"That's* the type of job I want," this trait almost always plays a central role. Once you understand this value of control, it changes the way you evaluate opportunities, leading you to consider a position's potential autonomy as being as important as its offered salary or the institution's reputation. This was the mindset I took into my own job search, and it helped me reenvision my choice between accepting Georgetown's offer or delaying it to go interview at the unnamed state university.

There were two important points I noticed when I started evaluating my options through the lens of control. First, Georgetown was just starting up its computer science PhD program as part of a more general campuswide investment in the sciences. Throughout my jobhunt process, my PhD advisor at MIT had been telling me about her experiences, early in her own career, working in Georgia Tech's computer science department during the period when it, too, was first transitioning toward a research-centric program. "In a growing program, you'll always have a say," she told me.

By contrast, at a well-established institution, your position in the hierarchy as a new assistant professor is clear: at the bottom. At these universities, you often have to wait until you're a full professor, years and years into your career, before you can start affecting the program's direction. Until this point you follow along with what gets passed down from on high.

The second thing I noticed was that Georgetown's tenure process was going to differ somewhat from the pattern of standard well-established programs. At a large research institution, tenure happens as follows: Higher-ups in the administration send out letters to other people in your general field and ask whether you're the top person in your particular specialty. If you're not, they'll fire you and try to hire whoever is. Some places go so far as to essentially tell their new hires not to expect tenure. (Academic-job markets are so tough, and with so much more available talent than open positions, they can get away with this.)

If your specialty is new—as mine is—and they can't therefore find experts with an opinion on it either way, you're going to have a real hard time keeping your position, as there's no one out there to validate your stature. Because of this, the system rewards conformity for junior faculty: That is, the safest route to tenure is to take a robust research topic that already has lots of interest and then outwork your peers. If you want to innovate, wait until later in your career. In his famed "Last Lecture," the late Carnegie Mellon computer science professor Randy Pausch captured this reality well when he quipped, "Junior faculty members used to come up to me and say, 'Wow, you got tenure early; what's your *secret?*' I said, 'It's pretty simple, call me any Friday night in my office at ten o'clock and I'll tell you.'"

Georgetown, by contrast, made it clear that they weren't interested in this explicit comparison-based approach to tenure. At this stage in its growth, the computer science department was more focused on developing star researchers than trying to hire them away. In other words, if I published good results in good venues, I could stay. Without pressure to choose a safe, preexisting area to dominate, I would therefore have much more flexibility in how my research program unfolded.

Viewed from the perspective of the control I would enjoy over my career, Georgetown was clearly more attractive than the well-established state university. Before finalizing my decision, however, I took some time to reflect on the other insights of Rule #3—insights that nuanced its otherwise enthusiastic endorsement of autonomy. During my quest, for example, I discovered two traps that typically trip people up in their search for control. The first trap was having too little career capital. If you go after more control in your working life without a rare and valuable skill to offer in return, you're likely pursuing a mirage.

This was the trap tripped, for example, by the many fans of lifestyle design, who left their traditional jobs to try to make a living on passive income-generating websites. Many of these contrarians quickly discovered that the income-generating piece of that plan doesn't work well if you don't have something valuable to offer in exchange for people's money. This trap might not seem relevant to my job hunt, as the academic-search process usually demands large stores of career capital—in the form of peer-reviewed publications and strong recommendation letters—before a candidate has a possibility of earning an offer. But there are departments lurking out there that will attract second-tier candidates (i.e., those without much career capital) with the allure of the autonomous academic life, but then, once they arrive on campus, saddle them with an overwhelming amount of teaching and service responsibilities. In other words, even in this rarefied world, one must still be wary of control mirages.

The second trap describes what happens when you *do* have enough capital to successfully make a shift toward more control. It's at this point that you're most likely to encounter resistance from others in your life, as more control usually benefits only *you*. Fortunately for me, my closest advisors at MIT encouraged me to pursue the flexibility offered by a fast-growing program like Georgetown's. But there were certainly those farther out in my professional orbit who were more resistant to this decision. To them, pounding a well-trod path at a well-established university was the safest route to the desired outcome of tenure and a good research reputation. The personal benefits of having more control over my work were not on their professional radar, so any decision outside the safe decision was deemed alarming.

While researching Rule #3, I came across a useful tool for navigating between these two traps. I called it *the law of financial viability,* and described it as follows: "When deciding whether to follow an appealing pursuit that will introduce more control into your work life, ask yourself whether people are willing to pay you for it. If so, continue. If not, move on."

Ultimately, this was the law that helped me finalize my own career decision. Georgetown offered much greater potential for control over what I did and how I did it. This seemed clear. Furthermore, they were willing to pay me well for this move toward autonomy, both financially and in terms of support for my research initiatives. According to the law of financial viability, I could therefore be confident that in going to Georgetown I would be avoiding both control traps: I had enough career capital to exchange for the potential flexibility and could confidently ignore the status quo–themed voices of resistance. So I turned down the interview request from the state university and held out for Georgetown.

How I Applied Rule #4

As explained in Rule #4, a career mission is an organizing purpose to your working life. It's what leads people to become famous for what they do and ushers in the remarkable opportunities that come along with such fame. It's also an idea that has long fascinated me.

Academia is a profession well suited for mission. If you identify professors with particularly compelling careers, and then ask what they did differently than their peers, the answer almost always involves them organizing their work around a catchy mission. Consider, for example, Alan Lightman, an MIT physics professor turned writer. Lightman started as a traditional physicist but was writing on the side—both fiction and nonfiction that grappled with the human side of science. He's perhaps best known for his bestselling, award-winning novel, *Einstein's Dreams*,[2] though he's written many other books, and his essays have appeared in basically every important American literary publication.

Lightman's career is based on his mission to explore the human side of science, and this led him to fascinating places. He left behind the grueling MIT physics tenure track to become the first professor in the Institute's history to be dual-appointed in both science and humanities. He helped develop MIT's communications requirement and then went on to found its graduate science-writing program. By the time I met Lightman, he had shifted to an adjunct-professor position, providing him even more freedom in his schedule, and had crafted for himself an impressively unburdened life of the mind. He now teaches writing courses that he designed and that focus on issues he thinks are important. He has freed himself from the need to be constantly seeking grant money or publications. He spends his summers with his family on an island in Maine—a location with no phone, TV, or Internet—presumably thinking big thoughts while basking in the sublimity of his surroundings. Most impressive to me, Lightman's contact page on his official MIT website gives the following disclaimer: "I don't use e-mail"—a move toward simplicity that a less famous academic would never get away with.

This is just one example among many of professors who leveraged mission to create an offbeat and compelling career. Some of these professors, such as Pardis Sabeti and Kirk French, I ended up tracking down and interviewing when researching this book, which is why you'll find the details of their stories in Rule #4. Others, such as Alan Lightman, or Erez Lieberman, who earned fame by the age of thirty-one through his combination of mathematics and cultural studies, or Esther Duflo, who won a MacArthur "Genius Grant" for her work evaluating ant-poverty programs, didn't make the cut for the book, but still weigh heavily on my thinking about how to best shape my own career.

It wasn't until I got started in earnest in my Rule #4 research, however, and met mission mavens such as Pardis, Kirk, and Giles Bowkett, that I understood just how tricky it is to make this trait a reality in your working life. The more you try to force it, I learned, the less likely you are to succeed. True missions, it turns out, require two things. First you need career capital, which requires patience. Second, you need to be ceaselessly scanning your always-changing view of the *adjacent possible* in your field, looking for the next big idea. This requires a dedication to brainstorming and exposure to new ideas. Combined, these two commitments describe a *lifestyle*, not a series of steps that automatically spit out a mission when completed. As I entered the summer of 2011, I leveraged this new understanding to try to transform my approach to work into one that would lead to a successful mission. These efforts generated a series of routines that I combined into a mission-development system. This system is best understood as a three-level pyramid. I'll explain each of these levels below.

Top Level: The Tentative Research Mission

My system is guided, at the top level of the pyramid, by a tentative research mission—a sort of rough guideline for the type of work I'm interested in doing. Right now, my mission reads, "To apply distributed algorithm theory to interesting new places with the goal of producing interesting new results." In order to identify this mission description, I had first to acquire career capital in my field. I've published and read enough distributed algorithm results to know that there's great potential in moving this body of theory to new settings. The real challenge, of course, is finding the compelling projects that exploit this potential. This is the goal the other two levels of the pyramid are designed to pursue.

Bottom Level: Background Research

We now dive from the top level of the pyramid to the bottom level, where we find my dedication to background research. Here's my rule: Every week, I expose myself to something new about my field. I can read a paper, attend a talk, or schedule a meeting. To ensure that I really understand the new idea, I require myself to add a summary, in my own words, to my growing "research bible" (which I introduced earlier in this conclusion when discussing how I applied Rule #2). I also try to carve out one walk each day for free-form thinking about the ideas turned up by this background research (I commute to work on foot and have a dog to exercise, so I have many such walks to choose from in my schedule). The choice of what material to expose myself to is guided by my mission description at the top of the pyramid.

This background-research process, which combines exposure to potentially relevant material with free-form re-combination of ideas, comes straight out of Steven Johnson's book, *Where Good Ideas Come From*, which I introduced in Rule #4 when talking about his notion of the adjacent possible. According to Johnson, access to new ideas and to the "liquid networks" that facilitate their mixing and matching often provides the catalyst for breakthrough new ideas.

Middle Level: Exploratory Projects

We arrive now at the middle level of the pyramid, which is responsible for most of the work I produce as a professor. As explained in Rule #4, an effective strategy for making the leap from a tentative mission idea to compelling accomplishments is to use small projects that I called "little bets" (borrowing the phrase from Peter Sims's 2010 book of the same title). As you might recall, a little bet, in the setting of mission exploration, has the following characteristics:

- It's a project small enough to be completed in less than a month.
- It forces you to create new value (e.g., master a new skill and produce new results that didn't exist before).
- It produces a concrete result that you can use to gather concrete feedback.

I use little bets to explore the most promising ideas turned up by the processes described by the bottom level of my pyramid. I try to keep only two or three bets active at a time so that they can receive intense attention. I also use deadlines, which I highlight in yellow in my planning documents, to help keep the urgency of their completion high. Finally, I also track my hours spent on these bets in the hour tally I described back in the section of this conclusion dedicated to my application of Rule #2. I found that without these accountability tools, I tended to procrastinate on this work, turning my attention to more urgent but less important matters.

When a little bet finishes, I use the concrete feedback it generates to guide my research efforts going forward. This feedback tells me, for example, whether a given project should be aborted and, if not, what direction is most promising to explore next. The effort of completing these bets also has the added side benefit of inducing deliberate practice—yet another tactic in my ever-growing playbook dedicated to making me better and better at what I do.

Ultimately, the success or failure of the projects pursued in this middle level helps me evolve the research mission maintained by the top level. In other words, the system as a whole is a closed feedback loop—constantly evolving toward a clearer and better supported vision for my work.

Final Thoughts: Working Right Trumps Finding the Right Work

This book opened with the story of Thomas, who believed that the key to happiness is to follow your passion. True to this conviction, he followed his passion for Zen practice to a remote monastery in the Catskill Mountains. Once there, he applied himself to the study of Zen, immersing himself in meditation and pondering endless Dharma lectures.

But Thomas didn't find the happiness he expected. He realized instead that although his surroundings had changed, he was "exactly the same person" as before he arrived at the monastery. The thought patterns that had previously convinced him, job after job, that he hadn't yet found his true calling had not disappeared. When we left Thomas back in this book's introduction, the weight of this realization had reduced him to tears. He sat in the quiet oak forest surrounding the monastery, crying.

Almost ten years later, I met Thomas at a coffee shop not far from my building at MIT. He was working in Germany at the time and was visiting Boston for a conference. Thomas is tall and slim with close-cropped hair. He wears the thin-framed square glasses that seem to be mandatory issue among European knowledge workers. As we sat and sipped coffee, Thomas filled me in on his life after his Zen crisis.

Here's what I learned: After leaving the monastery, Thomas returned to the banking job he had left two years earlier when he moved to the Catskills to pursue his passion. This time, however, he approached his working life with a new awareness. His experience at the monastery had freed him from the escapist thoughts of fantasy jobs that had once dominated his mind. He was able instead to focus on the tasks he was given and on accomplishing them well. He was free from the constant, draining comparisons he used to make between his current work and some magical future occupation waiting to be discovered.

This new focus, and the output it produced, was appreciated by management. Nine months into his job he was promoted. Then he was promoted again. And then again! Within two years he had moved from a lowly data-entry position to being put in charge of a computer system that managed over $6 billion of investment assets. By the time I met him, he had been put in charge of a system that manages five times that amount. His work is challenging, but Thomas enjoys the challenge. It also provides him with a sense of respect, impact, and autonomy—exactly the kind of rare and valuable traits, as you might recall, that I argued back in Rule #2 are needed for creating work you love. Thomas acquired these traits not by matching his work to his passion, but instead by doing his work well and then strategically cashing in the capital it generated.

Managing computer systems might not generate the daily bliss that defined Thomas's old daydreams, but as he now recognized, nothing would. A fulfilling working life is a more subtle experience than his old fantasies had allowed. As we chatted, Thomas agreed that a good way of describing his transformation is that he came to realize a simple truth: **Working right trumps finding the right work.** He didn't need to have a perfect job to find occupational happiness—he needed instead a better approach to the work already available to him.

I think it's fitting to end on Thomas's story, as it sums up the message at the core of this book: *Working right trumps finding the right work*—it's a simple idea, but it's also incredibly subversive, as it overturns decades of folk career advice all focused on the mystical value of passion. It wrenches us away from our daydreams of an overnight transformation into instant job bliss and provides instead a more sober way toward fulfillment. This is why I left this conclusion to Thomas's saga until the end of the book. I wanted the chance to first explore with you, through the four rules that came before, the nuances of "working right," providing example after example of how this approach can lead to increased enjoyment of your own working life. Now that you're armed with these insights, it's my hope that the end to Thomas's story is no longer so surprising.

I love what I do for a living. I'm also confident that as I continue my commitment to the ideas discovered in my quest, this love will only deepen. Thomas feels the same way about his work. So do most of the people I profiled in the book.

I want you to share in this confidence. To accomplish this goal, let the rules I uncovered guide you. Don't obsess over discovering your true calling. Instead, master rare and valuable skills. Once you build up the career capital that these skills generate, invest it wisely. Use it to acquire control over what you do and how you do it, and to identify and act on a life-changing mission. This philosophy is less sexy than the fantasy of dropping everything to go live among the monks in the mountains, but it's also a philosophy that has been shown time and again to actually work.

So next time you start to question whether you're missing out on some dream job waiting for you to muster the courage to pursue it, conjure up a pair of images. First, recall passion-obsessed Thomas, heartbroken and sobbing on the forest floor. Then replace this with the image of the smiling, confident, value-focused man who ten years later joined me for coffee—the version of Thomas who looked at me at one point in our conversation and remarked, without irony, "Life is good."

Glossary

A summary of the important terms, theories, and laws introduced in the book, presented in the order of their appearance.

the passion hypothesis (introduced in Rule #1): This hypothesis claims that the key to occupational happiness is to first figure out what you're passionate about and then find a job that matches this passion. The basic tenet behind this book is that the passion hypothesis, although widely believed, is both wrong and potentially dangerous.

"Be so good they can't ignore you." (introduced in Rule #2): A quote from comedian Steve Martin that captures what is needed to build a working life you love. It is excerpted from the following longer quote, which Martin gave in a 2007 interview with Charlie Rose when asked what his advice was for aspiring entertainers: "Nobody ever takes note of [my advice], because it's not the answer they wanted to hear. What they want to hear is 'Here's how you get an agent, here's how you write a script,'...but I always say, 'Be so good they can't ignore you.'"

the craftsman mindset (introduced in Rule #2): An approach to your working life in which you focus on the *value* of what you are offering to the world.

the passion mindset (introduced in Rule #2): An approach to your working life in which you focus on the value your job is offering you. This mindset stands in contrast to the craftsman mindset. The passion mindset ultimately leads to chronic dissatisfaction and daydreaming about the better jobs you imagine existing out there waiting to be discovered.

career capital (introduced in Rule #2): A description of the skills you have that are rare and valuable to the working world. This is the key currency for creating work you love.

the career capital theory of great work (introduced in Rule #2): This theory provides the foundation for all of the ideas that follow it in this book. It claims that the key to work you love is *not* to follow your passion, but instead to get good at something rare and valuable, and then cash in the "career capital" this generates to acquire the traits that define great jobs. This requires that you approach work with a craftsman mindset (focusing on your value to the world) and *not* a passion mindset (focusing on what value the world is offering you). Here is the formal three-part definition of the theory as presented in Rule #2:

- The traits that define great work are rare and valuable.
- Supply and demand says that if you want these traits, you need rare and valuable skills to offer in return. Think of these rare and valuable skills you can offer as your career capital.
- The craftsman mindset, with its relentless focus on being "so good they can't ignore you," is a strategy well suited for acquiring career capital. This is why it trumps the passion mindset if your goal is to have work you love.

the 10,000-hour rule (introduced in Rule #2): A rule, well-known to performance scientists, describing the amount of practice time required to master a skill. Malcolm Gladwell, who popularized the concept in his 2008 book *Outliers*, described it as follows: "The idea that excellence at performing a complex task requires a critical minimum level of practice surfaces again and again in studies of expertise. In fact, researchers have settled on what they believe is the magic number for true expertise: ten thousand hours."

deliberate practice (introduced in Rule #2): The style of difficult practice required to continue to improve at a task. Florida State University professor Anders Ericsson, who coined the term in the early 1990s, describes it formally as an "activity designed, typically by a teacher, for the sole purpose of effectively improving specific aspects of an individual's performance." Deliberate practice requires you to stretch past where you are comfortable and then receive ruthless feedback on your performance. In the context of career construction, most knowledge workers avoid this style of skill development because, quite frankly, it's uncomfortable. To build up large stores of career capital, however, which is necessary for creating work you love, you must make this style of practice a regular part of your work routine.

career capital markets (introduced in Rule #2): When acquiring career capital in a field, you can envision that you're acquiring this capital in a specific type of career capital market. There are two types of these markets: **winner-take-all** and **auction**.

In a winner-take-all market, there is only one type of career capital available and lots of different people competing for it. An auction market, by contrast, is less structured: There are many different types of career capital, and each person might generate their own unique collection of this capital. Different markets require different career capital acquisition strategies. In a winner-take-all market, for example, you need to first "crack the code" on how people master the one skill that matters. In an auction market, by contrast, you might simply emphasize rareness in the skill combinations that you create.

control (introduced in Rule #3): Control is having a say in what you do and how you do it. This is one of the most important traits to acquire with your career capital when creating work you love.

the first control trap (introduced in Rule #3): A warning to heed when trying to introduce more control into your working life. It represents the principle that control that's acquired *without* career capital is *not* sustainable.

the second control trap (introduced in Rule #3): Another warning to heed when trying to introduce more control into your working life. It represents the principle that when you acquire enough career capital to acquire meaningful control over your working life, that's exactly when you've become valuable enough to your current employer that they will try to prevent you from making the change.

courage culture (briefly introduced in Rule #2; elaborated in Rule #3): A term that describes the growing number of authors and online commentators who promote the idea that the only thing standing between you and a dream job is building the courage to step off the expected path.

Though well-intentioned, this culture is dangerous, as it underplays the importance of also having career capital to back up your career aspirations. It has led many people to quit their current job and to end up in a new situation where they are much worse off than before.

the law of financial viability (introduced in Rule #3): A simple law that can be deployed to help sidestep the two control traps when trying to introduce more control into your working life. It suggests that when deciding whether to follow an appealing pursuit that will introduce more control into your work life, you should ask yourself whether people are willing to pay for it. If so, continue. If not, move on.

mission (introduced in Rule #4): A mission is another important trait to acquire with your career capital when creating work you love. It provides a unifying goal for your career. It's more general than a specific job and can span multiple positions. It provides an answer to the question "What should I do with my life?"

the adjacent possible (introduced in Rule #4): A term taken from the science writer Steven Johnson, who took it from Stuart Kauffman, that helps explain the origin of innovation. Johnson notes that the next big ideas in any field are typically found right beyond the current cutting edge, in the adjacent space that contains the possible new combinations of existing ideas. The key observation is that you have to get to the cutting edge of a field before its adjacent possible—and the innovations it contains—becomes visible. In the context of career construction, it's important to note that good career missions are also often found in the adjacent possible. The implication, therefore, is that if you want to find a mission in your

career, you first need to get to the cutting edge of
your field.

little bets (introduced in Rule #4): An idea borrowed
from the business writer Peter Sims. When Sims studied innovative corporations and people, he noted
the following: "Rather than believing they have to
start with a big idea or plan out a whole project in
advance, they make a methodical series of *little bets*
about what might be a good direction, learning critical information from lots of little failures and from
small but significant wins" [emphasis mine]. In the
context of career construction, little bets provide a
good strategy for exploring productive ways to turn
a vague mission idea into specific successful projects.

the law of remarkability (introduced in Rule #4): A simple law that can help you identify successful projects
for making your mission a reality. (This can be used
in conjunction with the little-bets strategy.) The law
says that for a mission-driven project to succeed, it
should be "remarkable" in two different ways. First,
it must compel people who encounter it to remark
about it to others. Second, it must be launched in a
venue that supports such remarking.

Career Profile Summaries

A quick summary of the main career profiles from the book, presented in the order in which they appear.

JOE DUFFY

(introduced in Rule #2)

Current job:

Before recently retiring, Joe ran Duffy & Partners, his own fifteen-person branding and design shop.

Why he loves what he does:

He worked on handpicked international projects and was greatly respected (and rewarded) for his work. Between engagements he spent much of his time at Duffy Trails, a hundred-acre retreat he owns, tucked away on the banks of Wisconsin's Totagatic River.

How he applied the rules described in this book to get this job:

When Joe was starting out in his advertising career, like many at his young age, he chafed at the constraints of working for a large company. He had originally planned on being an artist and was entertaining the thought of quitting his job and returning to that "dream." Instead, Joe deployed career capital theory. He realized that the traits that define great work are rare and valuable and that therefore they require rare and valuable skills to be offered in return. He found a specialty within his field—brand communication through logos—and hunkered down to dominate the skill. He was hired away by a larger agency, which gave him more money and more freedom. As he continued to build career capital, they appeased him by allowing him to run an independent agency within the larger agency—providing Joe even more control. Eventually, he left to run his own shop on his own terms, using the monetary rewards of his expertise to buy Duffy Trails. Given that before he retired he controlled when he worked and what he worked on, he was able to get the most out of both his work and his relaxation.

ALEX BERGER

(introduced in Rule #2)

Current job:

Alex is a successful television writer.

Why he loves what he does:

When you're good enough to find a steady stream of work, television writing is a fantastic gig. It pays you loads of money to do highly creative projects that are seen by millions. In addition, it also gives you months off every year.

How he applied the rules described in this book to get this job:

When Alex first arrived in Hollywood, Ivy League diploma in hand, he thought he could break into the industry by launching and carefully managing a variety of different entertainment-related projects. It turned out that no one cared about his big ideas. It didn't take long for Alex to pare his attention down to a more specific pursuit: television writing. He realized that all that mattered in this field was a single type of career capital: the ability to write quality scripts.

Using the practice techniques honed as a college debate champion, he began to systematically improve his scriptwriting capability, sometimes working on as many as four or five writing projects at a time, while constantly exposing himself to ruthless feedback. This strategy paid off as his scriptwriting improved quickly, eventually earning him his first produced scripts, which in turn earned him his first staff writing jobs, which led to him cocreating a show with Michael Eisner. This is a classic example of career capital theory in action. To get a job he loved, Alex needed to first become so good that he couldn't be ignored.

MIKE JACKSON

(introduced in Rule #2)

Current job:

Mike is a director at the Westly Group, a cleantech venture capital firm on Silicon Valley's famous Sand Hill Road.

Why he loves what he does:

Clean-energy venture capital is a hot field. It offers a way to help the world while at the same time, as Mike admitted, "You make a lot of money."

How he applied the rules described in this book to get this job:

Mike didn't start with a clear vision of what he wanted to do with his life. He did understand, however, the basics of career capital theory: The more rare and valuable skills you have to offer, the more interesting opportunities will become available. With this in mind, Mike formed his early career around the goal of dominating one valuable pursuit after another, trusting that the large stores of career capital this would generate would lead him somewhere worth going. He started by choosing an ambitious master's thesis project that ended up making him an expert on international carbon markets. He then leveraged this expertise to run a green-energy start-up that sold carbon offsets contracts to American companies.

This combination of expert knowledge on green-energy markets and entrepreneurship experience made him a perfect match for the Westly Group, the clean-energy venture capital firm where he now works. Throughout this process, Mike's focus was on how to get better, not on figuring out his true calling. The result was an enviable job.

RYAN VOILAND

(introduced in Rule #3)

Current job:

Ryan, along with his wife, Sarah, runs Red Fire Farm, a thriving organic farm in Granby, Massachusetts.

Why he loves what he does:

Ryan has been training in horticulture since he was a teenager. To now own land that he can cultivate on his own terms is deeply fulfilling to him.

How he applied the rules described in this book to get this job:

Many people harbor a rosy image of farm life. They imagine it would be nice to spend time outdoors in nice weather and be free from the distractions of the modern office. Spend time with Ryan at Red Fire, however, and this myth is quickly dispelled. Farming, it turns out, is hard work. The weather is not something you enjoy, as if on vacation, but instead a force poised to play havoc with your crops. And far from being free from modern distractions, a farmer is a businessman, with all the e-mail, Excel spreadsheets, and QuickBooks software that come along with that role. The reason Ryan loves what he does, it turns out, is not that he gets to be outside or be free from e-mail, but instead that he has *control*—over both what he does and how he does it.

This trait, as described in Rule #3, is crucial for creating work you love. What's important about Ryan's story is that he didn't just decide one day that farming would provide nice control and then go buy some land. Instead, he recognized that control, like any valuable career trait, requires career capital to acquire. With this in mind, he built up his farming skills for over a decade before setting out on his own. It started with cultivating his parents' garden and selling produce by the road. From there, he slowly built up his abilities by taking on larger cultivation projects. By the time he left for Cornell to study horticulture, he was renting land from a local farmer. It wasn't until after he earned his degree that he applied for a loan for his first parcel of land. Given his expertise, it's not surprising that his new farm thrived. He's a perfect example of both the value of control and the patient capital acquisition required before you can gain this trait in your working life.

LULU YOUNG

(introduced in Rule #3)

Current job:

Lulu is a freelance software developer.

Why she loves what she does:

Lulu enjoys challenging software projects, but she also enjoys having control over her life, including when she works, what she works on, and under what terms. As a freelance developer with skills that are in high demand, she has been able to maintain that control, allowing her to mix her work with a variety of different leisurely pursuits, from monthlong trips to Asia, to pilot's training, to weekday afternoons spent with her nephew.

How she applied the rules described in this book to get this job:

Lulu, like Ryan, is a good example of the value of control. Also like Ryan, she's a good example of leveraging career capital in pursuit of this trait. Lulu didn't decide out of the blue to be a freelance developer; instead she built up her skills and reputation over many years in the industry. She now has more than enough career capital to set her own terms for her work. When you study her story, however, you learn that this shift toward increased autonomy didn't happen all at once. Instead, Lulu developed a steady stream of bids for increased freedom as she got increasingly good at what she did.

It started with her first job as a software tester—the bottom of the developer heap. Lulu figured out how to automate much of the testing process. The capital this generated allowed her to then bargain for a thirty-hour workweek so she could take philosophy classes on the side. As she got even better at what she did, she invested her growing capital stores in obtaining positions at a series of start-ups, where she was given more and more control over her work. It was after one of these start-ups was acquired by a large company, which promptly added new constraints, that Lulu transitioned to a freelance role. At this point, however, her career capital stores were more than sufficient to support this final bid for even more control.

DEREK SIVERS

(introduced in Rule #3)

Current job:

Derek is an entrepreneur, writer, and thinker.

Why he loves what he does:

Derek has had enough successes in his career that he can now live where he wants and work on projects he finds interesting when he decides he's in the mood to work. He's in complete control over his life and is taking full advantage of this autonomy.

How he applied the rules described in this book to get this job:

Derek is another example of control being a defining trait of a great career. What made him most relevant to our discussion in Rule #3, however, is the rule he deploys when deciding whether or not to pursue a bid for more autonomy. I called this rule "the law of financial viability," and it says that you should only pursue a project if people are willing to pay you for it. If they aren't, you probably don't have sufficient capital to exchange for the control you desire.

This is the law that helped guide Derek to his current levels of success. He first applied it when deciding to quit his job at Warner Bros. to become a full-time musician. He delayed this decision until the money he was making from music was equal to what he made in his day job—if he couldn't get to this modest level of income with part-time playing, he reasoned, then he was unlikely to enjoy enough success pursuing this career full-time. He next applied the law when starting CD Baby, the company he eventually sold for millions. He didn't drop everything to pursue his entrepreneurial ambition. Instead, he started small. When the company made a little money, he used this money to expand it so it could make a little more. When it started to make a lot of money, only then did he decide to make it into his full-time job.

The courage culture pushes us to make drastic bids for increased control over our working lives. Derek's example provides a nice reality check. Seeking freedom is good, but it's easy to fail in this pursuit. The law of financial viability provides a good guide past these pitfalls.

PARDIS SABETI

(introduced in Rule #4)

Current job:

Pardis is a professor of evolutionary biology at Harvard University.

Why she loves what she does:

Pardis's academic career is built around a mission that she finds both exciting and important: to use computational genetics to help rid the world of ancient diseases.

How she applied the rules described in this book to get this job:

Pardis is a good example of the value of organizing your working life around a compelling mission. Many professors are overwhelmed by their jobs and eventually descend into a state of bitter cynicism. Pardis avoided this fate by dedicating her work toward something she finds important and exciting. Of equal importance is how she found her mission. Many people incorrectly believe that coming up with a mission is the easy part (it's something that just happens in a moment of inspiration) and that what's hard is mustering the courage to pursue it. Rule #4 argued the opposite. It said that real missions—those that you can build a career around—require that you build up extensive amounts of expertise before they can be identified.

Once they are identified, however, pursuing them is often a no-brainer. This is exactly what we find in the story of Pardis. It took years of skill acquisition before Pardis was able to identify the mission that now defines her career. After college she went on to earn her PhD in genetics. Not quite sure what she wanted to do with her life, she *also* went to medical school. It wasn't until after finishing medical school and spending time as a postdoctoral fellow that she finally had enough expertise in her field to sift out this exciting new opportunity. Overall, Pardis's most important commitment was to patience. She didn't try to force a direction for her working life, but instead built up her career capital and kept her eyes open for the interesting directions she knew this process would uncover.

KIRK FRENCH

(introduced in Rule #4)

Current job:

Kirk teaches archaeology at Penn State University and is the cohost of a television show on the Discovery Channel that lets him travel the country helping people figure out the historical importance of their keepsakes and heirlooms.

Why he loves what he does:

As a teacher, Kirk has long been interested in spreading the word about modern archaeology. Ever since being interviewed for a documentary on the Mayan culture (Kirk's specialty), he has also been interested in media as a vehicle for popularizing archaeology. Landing a television show has been a fantastic realization of these interests.

How he applied the rules described in this book to get this job:

Kirk organized his archaeological career around the mission of popularizing his field. This mission has helped him turn an academic career that could become dry or overwhelming into a source of adventure and fulfillment. As with Pardis, this mission first required career capital—in Kirk's case, this came in the form of his PhD. His story, however, also highlights the first of two strategies presented in Rule #4 for helping career missions, once they're identified, succeed.

The idea to host a television show did not come to Kirk out of the blue. Instead, he explored his general mission idea—to popularize archaeology—by means of a series of "little bets." Many of these, such as his attempts to raise finances for a documentary, failed, but these failures were important, as they helped Kirk shift his attention away from non-productive directions. In the end, it was one of these bets that led him directly to his television show. He decided to film a visit to a local man who claimed to have found the Knights Templars' treasure buried in his suburban Pittsburgh property.

Not long afterward, a producer wrote Kirk's department chair looking for ideas for an archaeology-related television show. Kirk saw the e-mail and sent the producer his Knights Templar tape. The producer loved it, and not long after, a show concept was born with Kirk as the host. Building the expertise to identify a quality career mission is the first step toward leveraging this trait. As Kirk's story demonstrated, deploying a series of little bets to feel out the best way forward with this mission is a good second step.

GILES BOWKETT

(introduced in Rule #4)

Current job:

Giles is a well-known Ruby software programmer. His renown has allowed him to shift between many jobs, following his interest of the moment. He's worked for the country's top Ruby shop, supported himself entirely off of blog income, helped a Hollywood movie star launch a Web-based entertainment venture, and, most recently, started writing a book.

Why he loves what he does:

Because Giles has a hyperkinetic personality, his ability to jump from one interesting job to another, moving on once something becomes boring, is a perfect match for his rapidly shifting attention. Spend any time around Giles and you'll realize how miserable he would be if forced by economic necessity into a long-term, traditional, forty-hour-a-week job.

How he applied the rules described in this book to get this job:

Giles is another example of mission being used as the foundation for a great career. In this case, the mission is combining the worlds of the arts and Ruby programming. Giles made this mission a success when he released Archaeopteryx, an open-source software program that writes and performs its own music. This software gave Giles the fame within his community that has supported his kinetic career trajectory ever since.

Like Pardis and Kirk, Giles needed career capital before he could identify his mission. He seriously studied and performed music and spent many years developing his programming skills before he was at a sufficient level of expertise to recognize the potential in combining these worlds. His story, however, also captures the second of the two strategies presented in Rule #4 for helping missions, once identified, to succeed. This second strategy, which I called "the law of remarkability," says that a good mission-driven project should be remarkable in two ways: First, it should compel people to remark about it, and second, it should be deployed in a venue conducive to remarking. These were the rules that led Giles to his idea for Archaeopteryx. He recognized that a demo of a piece of computer code generating sophisticated music would be something that would catch people's attention. He had also realized that the open-source software community was well structured to spread the word about interesting projects, making it a perfect venue for the software's release. Combined, these two traits made the project, and therefore Giles's career mission, a success.

Acknowledgments

The decision to write this book can be traced back to a series of posts on the passion hypothesis that I first published on my blog, *Study Hacks*. The reaction from my readers was immediate and voluminous. Their feedback helped shape and focus my thinking on this topic and convinced me that this was a discussion worth sharing with a wider audience. As such, I thank them for spurring me into starting this project.

It was at this point that my publishing team entered the picture. My longtime agent and mentor, Laurie Abkemeier, worked her magic and helped me transform my diverse thoughts into a cohesive book proposal. The book ended up with Rick Wolff at Grand Central/Business Plus, and I couldn't be happier about this turn of events. Rick is the type of editor authors hope for. He understood my idea at a gut level, and his enthusiasm for it never waned. He helped me find the right voice for expressing these provocative arguments in a way that people would accept. The book is indisputably better due to his efforts.

Finally, my wife, Julie, was indispensable in the

writing process. She not only read drafts of my work in progress but also listened through endless iterations of my thinking, always offering honest and clear feedback. She was joined in these efforts by my friend Ben Casnocha, who conceived, sold, and wrote a career-advice book concurrently with my own, allowing us to share numerous useful conversations at all stages of the process.

Notes

Chapter 2: Passion Is Rare

1. Roadtrip Nation, http://roadtripnation.com. If you click on the "Watch" link, you can browse the PBS series by season, and within each season browse each episode by the interview subjects.
2. Interview with Ira Glass, Roadtrip Nation Online Episode Archive, 2005, http://roadtripnation.com/IraGlass.
3. Interview with Andrew Steele, Roadtrip Nation Online Episode Archive, 2005, http://roadtripnation.com/AndrewSteele.
4. Interview with Al Merrick, Roadtrip Nation Online Episode Archive, 2004, http://roadtripnation.com/AlMerrick.
5. Interview with William Morris, Roadtrip Nation Online Episode Archive, 2006, http://roadtripnation.com/WilliamMorris.
6. Vallerand, Blanchard, Mageau et al., *"Les passions de l'âme*: On Obsessive and Harmonious Passion," *Journal of Personality and Social Psychology* 85, no. 4 (2003): 756–67.
7. Wrzesniewski, McCauley, Rozin, et al., "Jobs, Careers, and Callings: People's Relations to Their Work," *Journal of Research in Personality* 31 (1997): 21–33.
8. See the following for an academic overview: Deci and Ryan, "The 'What' and 'Why' of Goal Pursuits: Human Needs and the Self-Determination of Behavior," *Psychological Inquiry* 11 (2000): 227–68. For more popular coverage, see Daniel Pink's book, *Drive: The Surprising Truth About What Motivates Us* (New York: Riverhead, 2009), or the official website for the theory: http://www.psych.rochester.edu/SDT/.

Chapter 3: Passion Is Dangerous

1. Daniel H. Pink, "What Happened to Your Parachute?" Fast-Company.com, August 31, 1999, http://www.fastcompany.com /magazine/27/bolles.html.
2. Google Books Ngram Viewer, http://books.google.com/ ngrams.
3. Arnett, "Oh, Grow Up! Generational Grumbling and the New Life Stage of Emerging Adulthood—Commentary on Trzesniewski & Donnellan (2010)," *Perspectives on Psychological Science* 5, no. 1 (2010): 89–92. See section titled "Slackers or Seekers of Identity-Based Work?" for the quote and related discussion.
4. Julianne Pepitone, "U.S. job satisfaction hits 22-year low," CNNMoney.com, January 5, 2010, http://money.cnn.com/2010 /01/05/news/economy/job_satisfaction_report/.
5. Alexandra Robbins and Abby Wilner, *Quarterlife Crisis: The Unique Challenges of Life in Your Twenties* (New York: Tarcher, 2001).
6. Interview with Peter Travers, Roadtrip Nation Online Video Archive, 2006, http://roadtripnation.com/PeterTravers.

Chapter 4: The Clarity of the Craftsman

1. George Graham, "The Graham Weekly Album Review #1551: Jordan Tice: *Long Story*," George Graham's Weekly Album Reviews, March 11, 1999, http://georgegraham.com/reviews /tice.html.
2. Steve Martin, *Born Standing Up: A Comic's Life* (New York: Scribner, 2007).
3. "An Hour with Steve Martin" (originally aired on PBS, December 12, 2007), available online at: http://www.charlierose.com /view/interview/8831.
4. Steve Martin, "Being Funny: How the pathbreaking comedian got his act together," *Smithsonian*, February 2008, available online at: http://www.smithsonianmag.com/arts-culture /funny-martin-200802.html.
5. Calvin Newport, "The Steve Martin Method: A Master Comedian's Advice for Becoming Famous," Study Hacks (blog),

February 1, 2008, http://calnewport.com/blog/2008/02/01/the-steve-martin-method-a-master-comedians-advice-for-becoming-famous/.

6. Po Bronson, "What Should I Do with My Life?" FastCompany.com, December 31, 2002, http://www.fastcompany.com/magazine/66/mylife.html.

7. Po Bronson, *What Should I Do With My Life: The True Story of People Who Answered the Ultimate Question* (New York: Random House, 2002).

Chapter 5: The Power of Career Capital

1. "Ira Glass on Storytelling, part 3 and 4," YouTube video, 5:20, video courtesy of Current TV, uploaded by "PRI" on August 18, 2009, http://www.youtube.com/watch?v=BI23U7U2aUY.

2. Kelly Slater, "Al Merrick Talks Sleds," Channel Island Surfboards (blog), January 6, 2011, http://cisurfboards.com/blog/2011/al-merrick-talks-sleds/.

3. Emily Bazelon, "The Self-Employed Depression," *New York Times Magazine*, June 7, 2009, page MM38, available online at: http://www.nytimes.com/2009/06/07/magazine/07unemployed-t.html.

4. Pamela Slim, *Escape from Cubicle Nation: From Corporate Prisoner to Thriving Entrepreneur* (New York: Portfolio Hardcover, 2009).

5. Pamela Slim, "Rebuild Your Backbone. Because you are good enough, smart enough, and doggonit, people like you," Escape From Cubicle Nation (author's website), http://www.escapefromcubiclenation.com/rebuild-your-backbone-because-you-are-good-enough-smart-enough-and-doggonit-people-like-you/.

6. Stephen Regenold, "A Retreat Groomed to Sate a Need to Ski," *New York Times*, June 5, 2009, C34, available online at: http://www.nytimes.com/2009/06/05/greathomesanddestinations/05Away.html.

7. For more details on the dangers of this particular trap, see Robert I. Sutton, *The No Asshole Rule: Building a Civilized Workplace and Surviving One That Isn't* (New York: Warner Business Books, 2007).

Chapter 6: The Career Capitalists

1. "Salon Media Circus," Salon.com, October 1997. Between the research and editing phases of this book, the online version of this column seems to have been taken offline. It was originally available at: http://www.salon.com/media/1997/10/29money.html.

Chapter 7: Becoming a Craftsman

1. Djakow, Petrowski, and Rudik, *Psychologie des Schachspiels [Psychology of Chess]* (Berlin: Walter de Gruyter, 1927).
2. Charness, Tuffiash, Krampe, et al., "The Role of Deliberate Practice in Chess Expertise," *Applied Cognitive Psychology* 19, no. 2 (2005): 151–65.
3. Malcolm Gladwell, *Outliers: The Story of Success* (New York: Little, Brown and Company, 2008).
4. http://www.psy.fsu.edu/faculty/ericsson/ericsson.exp.perf .html.
5. Ericsson and Lehmann, "Expert and Exceptional Performance: Evidence of Maximal Adaptation to Task Constraints," *Annual Review of Psychology* 47 (1996): 273–305.
6. Ericsson, Anders K. "Expert Performance and Deliberate Practice," http://www.psy.fsu.edu/faculty/ericsson/ericsson.exp.perf .html.
7. Geoff Colvin, *Talent Is Overrated: What Really Separates World-Class Performers from Everybody Else* (New York: Portfolio Hardcover, 2008).
8. Geoff Colvin, "Why talent is overrated," CNNMoney.com, October 21, 2008 (originally appeared in *Fortune*), http://money .cnn.com/2008/10/21/magazines/fortune/talent_colvin.fortune /index.htm.

Chapter 8: The Dream-Job Elixir

1. Daniel H. Pink, *Drive: The Surprising Truth About What Motivates Us* (New York: Riverhead Hardcover, 2009).
2. DeCharms, "Personal Causation Training in the Schools," *Journal of Applied Social Psychology* 2, no. 2 (1972): 95–112.
3. "ROWE Business Case," Results-Only Work Environment (ROWE) website, http://gorowe.com/wordpress/wp-content/ uploads/2009/12/ROWE-Business-Case.pdf.

Chapter 11: Avoiding the Control Freaks

1. "Derek Sivers: How to start a movement," TED.com, video posted online April 2010, http://www.ted.com/talks/derek_ sivers_how_to_start_a_movement.html.

Chapter 12: The Meaningful Life of Pardis Sabeti

1. "Pardis Sabeti: Expert Q & A," NOVA ScienceNOW, posted July 7, 2008, http://www.pbs.org/wgbh/nova/body/sabeti-genet ics-qa.html.

Chapter 13: Missions Require Capital

1. Steven Johnson, *Where Good Ideas Come From: The Natural History of Innovation* (New York: Riverhead Hardcover, 2010).
2. Sabeti, Reich, Higgens, et al., "Detecting recent positive selection in the human genome from haplotype structure," *Nature* 419 no. 6909 (2002): 832–837.

Chapter 14: Missions Require Little Bets

1. Kirk and Jason hated this name, as it goes against the tenets of archaeology to assign financial value to artifacts. They much preferred their original suggestion of *Artifact or Fiction*. In an ironic twist, after airing just three episodes of the first season, the Discovery Channel was sued by an individual who claimed to own the rights to *American Treasure*. They pulled the series from the air that summer and planned to re-air it the following summer, this time using Kirk and Jason's original title suggestion.
2. Peter Sims, *Little Bets: How Breakthrough Ideas Emerge from Small Discoveries* (New York: Free Press, 2011).

Chapter 15: Missions Require Marketing

1. Seth Godin, *Purple Cow: Transform Your Business by Being Remarkable* (New York: Portfolio Hardcover, 2003).
2. Seth Godin, "In Praise of the Purple Cow," FastCompany.com, January 31, 2003, http://www.fastcompany.com/magazine/67 /purplecow.html.
3. Chad Fowler, *My Job Went to India: 52 Ways to Save Your Job* (Pragmatic Programmers) (Raleigh, NC: Pragmatic Bookshelf, 2005).

Conclusion

1. The necessity and difficulty of these problem sets in learning mathematics is one of the reservations I have about the growing self-education movement. Without someone to grade your problem-set results—a grade that might play a big role in what options are available to you in the future—it's hard to imagine repeatedly pushing yourself through the dozens of hours of strain required to get yourself to answers, and in turn experience substantial skill growth.

2. Alan Lightman, *Einstein's Dreams* [paperback] (New York: Vintage, 2004).

Index

About the Author

CAL NEWPORT is an Assistant Professor of Computer Science at Georgetown University. He previously earned his PhD from MIT and his bachelor's from Dartmouth College.

Newport is the author of three books of unconventional advice for students: *How to Be a High School Superstar*, *How to Become a Straight-A Student*, and *How to Win at College*. He runs the popular blog, Study Hacks, which decodes patterns of success for both students and graduates.

He lives with his wife in Washington, D.C. Visit him at www.calnewport.com.